Jack London

Titles in the series Critical Lives present the work of leading cultural figures of the modern period. Each book explores the life of the artist, writer, philosopher or architect in question and relates it to their major works.

In the same series

# Jack London

Kenneth K. Brandt

REAKTION BOOKS

*For my parents, Shirley and Dr James K. Brandt*

Published by
REAKTION BOOKS LTD
Unit 32, Waterside
44–48 Wharf Road
London N1 7UX, UK

www.reaktionbooks.co.uk

First published 2021
Copyright © Kenneth K. Brandt 2021

Printed and bound in Great Britain by Bell & Bain, Glasgow

A catalogue record for this book is available from the British Library

ISBN 978 1 78914 387 4

# Contents

'I intend to live forever and to be always young.' Jack London writing in the outdoors, 1905.

# 1

# Western Youth: Born into the Underclass (1875–88)

. . . all things bear the imprint of the moment they are born.
Benson Bobrick[1]

I had lived my childhood on California ranches, my boyhood hustling newspapers on the streets of a healthy Western city, and my youth on the ozone-laden waters of San Francisco Bay.
Jack London[2]

Who is the father? The question of Jack London's paternity will probably never be definitively answered. The preponderance of evidence, though, sways heavily towards a man named William H. Chaney. Late in the spring of 1875, London's mother, Flora Wellman, was living with Chaney in the city of San Francisco. He was 54, she was 31. It is unlikely that they were ever legally married, but they lived together as Mr and Mrs Chaney in Mrs Upstone's lodging house. The residence was respectable though not elegant. What drew them together was a consuming interest in the occult and a shared passion for progressive ideas. Chaney was an astrologer and Flora was a spiritualist. He specialized in birth horoscopes, while she could purportedly reconnect you with your dead relatives. Eccentrics for sure, but not so different from many other wayfarers in the 1870s who were drawn to the ever-expanding, eclectic metropolis of San Francisco. The couple associated with a coterie of freethinkers whose chief organ was a periodical entitled *Common Sense: A Journal of Live Ideas*. This publication espoused a potpourri of reformist platforms aimed at advancing liberal causes, including women's suffrage, free love, civil rights and labour reform.

Chaney and Flora were together for about a year when their bohemian lives were suddenly complicated by Flora's becoming pregnant. When she informed Chaney, he became irate. A brutal and drawn-out argument ensued. He vehemently claimed that he could not be the father because he was 'impotent', and, besides that, Flora had had other lovers. He demanded she get an abortion. She refused. The child, later to become known to the world as the celebrated author Jack London, would be 21 before he learned of this scandal, at which time he wrote to Chaney questioning his paternity. The astrologer, by then 76 years old, denied everything, responding, 'I was never married to Flora Wellman, but she lived with me from June 11, 1874, until June 3, 1875. I was impotent at that time, the result of hardship, privation and too much brain-work. Therefore I cannot be your father, nor am I sure who your father is.'[3] He added that 'a very loose connection of society was fashionable . . . at that time' and reiterated his old claim that Flora had been with other men.[4] Back in 1875, Chaney had steadfastly denied any responsibility for Flora's pregnancy, and after her refusal to have an abortion, he abandoned her. Distraught, she twice attempted suicide – first with laudanum, and then with a double-barrelled pistol. The laudanum did not take and the pistol shot merely grazed the side of her forehead, which was fortunate for Flora and subsequently for American literature.

The couple's feud soon erupted into a public brouhaha through a series of sensational newspaper articles. The *San Francisco*

Studio portrait of Flora Wellman, *c.* 1870, photographic print.

*Chronicle* reported the scurrilous affair with headlines that read 'A DISCARDED WIFE: WHY MRS. CHANEY TWICE ATTEMPTED SUICIDE. Driven from Home for Refusing to Destroy her Unborn Infant – A Chapter of Heartlessness and Domestic Misery.' The article went on to divulge that

> [Chaney] told her she had better destroy her unborn babe.
> This she indignantly declined to do, and . . . he said to her,
> 'Flora, I want you to pack up and leave this house.' She replied,
> 'I have no money and nowhere to go.' He said, 'Neither
> have I any to give you.' A woman in the house offered her
> $25, but she flung it from her in a burst of anguish, saying,
> 'What do I care for this? It will be of no use to me without
> my husband's love.' . . . He told the poor woman that he had

sold the furnishings (for which she had helped to pay) and it was useless to think of her remaining there any longer.[5]

Luridly, the article continues: 'He then left her, and shortly after she made her first attempt at suicide, following it by the effort to kill herself with a pistol on the following morning . . . Failing in both endeavors, Mrs Chaney was removed in a half-insane condition . . . to the house of a friend.'[6] According to Chaney, a mob of 150 people gathered, 'swearing to hang me from the nearest lamppost'.[7] He eventually relocated to Oregon and never communicated with Flora again.

Despite his disavowals, Chaney remains the most likely candidate for London's biological father.[8] Movement and restlessness characterize the life of this obviously intelligent but

Portrait engraving of astrologer William Henry Chaney, 1890.

chronically restive man. Born in Maine on 13 January 1821, Chaney took to the sea on a fishing schooner at age sixteen to escape the drudgery of farm work. He spent nine months in the navy and had visions of joining up with pirates on the Mississippi and the Gulf of Mexico. The reality of the next few years was not as swashbuckling as he had originally envisioned. He spent time as a store clerk, a journalist and a lawyer. Chaney was frequently prone to altering his ideas on politics, religion and morality, but he honed in hard on astrology, which he called 'the most precious science ever made known to man', and dubbed himself 'Professor' W. H. Chaney.[9] Though it might be tempting to see him as a kind of mountebank, he was actually an innovative and rigorous thinker who dispensed with much of the quackery associated with astrological studies and made significant contributions to the profession – a field that was taken more seriously in his era than today. By all accounts, if idiosyncratic and cantankerous, Chaney was also sincerely dedicated to the betterment of human society. His reformist spirit and a cavalier rejection of convention were attractive qualities to Flora, who had spurned the comforts and confines of her privileged upbringing.

Flora Wellman, born on 17 August 1843, was the youngest child in an affluent family from Massillon, Ohio. Her father, Marshall Wellman, was a successful contractor, canal builder and trader. He was known as the 'Wheat King'. Flora enjoyed a pampered childhood. She grew up in a stylish seventeen-room mansion with the benefits of private tutors, music lessons and elegant clothes. At thirteen, she was stricken with typhoid fever, and the illness caused extensive permanent hair loss, damaged her eyesight and stunted her growth – as an adult she was well under 1.5 metres (5 ft) tall. She left home at sixteen and after the Civil War wandered west to Seattle and later to San Francisco. An accomplished pianist and talented seamstress, she eked out a living giving music and elocution lessons and taking in sewing, but her passion was spiritualism, and she

Jennie Prentiss standing in the doorway of a house, *c.* 1880. Jack London is the boy with a hat, sitting on the right.

conducted seances over the years in which she acted as a medium through which the living allegedly spoke to the dead.

After Chaney deserted her, Flora lived with Amanda and William Slocum, the publishers of *Common Sense*. She gave birth to the future author on 12 January 1876, and named him John Griffith Chaney. (John Griffith was a nephew.) The birth was arduous and left the already fragile Flora depleted. She was unable to produce enough milk for her newborn and needed to find a wet nurse.

The day Flora gave birth, a local African American woman named Virginia 'Jennie' Prentiss delivered a stillborn daughter. Due to Flora's weakened condition and difficulties lactating, the doctor (also Flora's physician) arranged for Jennie to become London's wet nurse. For at least the first nine months, and likely through the first two years of his life, London lived primarily with the Prentisses. He was lavishly nurtured by Jennie, who became his foster mother and called him her 'Jumping Jack'. Meanwhile, Flora, whose natural disposition was, outwardly at least, notably reserved and aloof, was more consumed with regaining social status than parenting. In contrast to Flora, who referred to London as her 'badge of shame', Jennie was generously affectionate and loving throughout his childhood and provided the wellspring of adoration that Flora did not display towards her own son.[10] Even after he was weaned, the young London made frequent visits to the Prentiss household, but oftentimes had to dodge other neighbourhood children who were physically hostile because of his attachment to an African American family. In 1903 London inscribed a copy of his *The People of the Abyss* for Jennie, signing it: 'Your Son, Jack'.[11] Years later, Jennie helped care for London's daughters, and she even nursed Flora in her old age. After he became a successful author, London bought Jennie a house, gave her financial support and provided for her in his will.

Jennie was a former slave who had fled the South during the Civil War and married Alonzo Prentiss. Alonzo was of mixed European and African ancestry and had previously been married to a white woman while he was a Union soldier in the Civil War. When knowledge of his mixed heritage surfaced during the war, his marriage disintegrated and, despite a commendable service record, he was discharged from the army. Jennie and Alonzo moved to Oakland, where he worked as a carpenter. Resolutely proud of her African racial identity, Jennie was a community and church leader. The Prentisses had two children and lived a stable middle-class life. Alonzo, who was fair-skinned, often passed for white to work a variety of carpentry jobs. Though construction work was plentiful in the ever-expanding Bay Area, non-whites were regularly excluded from the mainstream workforce. From the start, London's life had a significant cross-ethnic and multicultural dimension, and early on he became aware of the social complexities and dangers of moving back and forth across racial boundaries.

It was also through the Prentisses that Flora ended up meeting a man named John London, who had worked with Alonzo as a

John London, *c.* 1890, photographic print.

carpenter. It happened that John London was impressed with the quality of one of Alonzo's shirts that Flora had sewn and asked where he could get one. The Prentisses introduced him to Flora, they found each other suitably compatible, and were married on 7 September 1876, eight months after London's birth. Following her marriage to John London, she renamed the child John Griffith London. He was known as Johnny throughout his childhood, but in adolescence he would adopt the brisker nickname Jack.

After John London's first wife died of tuberculosis in 1873, he headed to California, seeking a new start, with three of his children: Charles, Eliza and Ida. Charles died soon after they arrived, and John had to place eight-year-old Eliza and five-year-old Ida in an orphanage while he sought work in San Francisco. He was able to get work as a carpenter and pay for his children's stay at the orphanage, but marrying Flora would provide the domestic stability he needed to reunite his family. Though lacking a romantic spark, marriage with Flora offered a sensible arrangement for all parties involved.

Born on 11 January 1828, John London was 48 years old when he married 33-year-old Flora. Raised on a farm in Pennsylvania, he had worked variously as a railroad foreman, farmer, Union Civil War soldier, frontiersman and carpenter. London described him as 'a soldier, scout, backwoodsman, trapper, and wanderer'.[12] During the Civil War he served with the 126th Illinois Volunteers and survived serious bouts of the measles and pneumonia, which permanently damaged his lungs. 'Despite physical limitations,' Clarice Stasz notes, 'John London represented an iconic American type: the frontier man who survived by his own wile and guts. Jack's exceptional confidence in his ability to achieve any goal could be rooted in London's role model.'[13] With his first wife, John London had meandered about the Midwest in a prairie schooner, eventually homesteading near Moscow, Iowa, where he hunted, trapped and farmed. He also traded with the Pawnee people and learned their

Jack London at age nine, *c.* 1885.

language.[14] He was a caring parent who indelibly shaped London's early years. Even after he learned about Chaney, London publicly maintained that John London was his father. This move shielded him from being denounced as a bastard and bolstered his 'all-American' image, but it also indicates his deep and genuine respect for John London. 'My father', he maintained, 'was the best man I have ever known' and was 'too intrinsically good to get ahead in the soulless scramble for a living that a man must cope with if he would survive in our anarchical capitalist system'.[15] John London introduced his son to fishing, boating and bird hunting on San Francisco Bay and nearby estuaries. He also entertained him with stories of the Civil War and regaled him with pioneer lore. Plus, he acquainted his young son with the hearty male-only ambiance of saloons. 'My one greatest regret, always,' London later said, 'is that my father could not live to share my prosperity.'[16] Though he was an industrious and versatile worker, John London's physical condition worsened as he aged, and by the late 1880s he was reduced to working as a deputy constable and Oakland port night watchman.

Looking back on his early years, the defining theme for London was a pervasive feeling of deprivation. 'My environment', he wrote, 'was crude and rough and raw. I had no outlook, but an uplook rather. My place in society was at the bottom. Here life offered nothing but sordidness and wretchedness, both of the flesh and the spirit; for here flesh and spirit were alike starved and tormented.'[17] Descriptions of hunger, poverty and crudity saturate recollections of his youth. 'My body and soul were starved when I was a child,' he lamented. In an 1898 letter, London declares:

> When I was seven years old, at the country school of San Pedro, this happened. Meat, I was that hungry for it I once opened a girl's basket and stole a piece of meat – a little piece the size of my two fingers . . . In those days, like Esau, I would have literally sold my birthright for a mess of pottage, a piece of meat. Great God! When those youngsters threw chunks of meat on the ground because of surfeit, I could have dragged it from the dirt and eaten it, but I did not. Just imagine the development of my mind, my soul, under such material conditions. This meat incident is an epitome of my whole life.[18]

Not so improbably, meat would become a common thematic focus in his mature writing. As the fundamental restorer of life force, it is the ideal naturalistic trope because meat is life and life is meat. Let the fanciful romancers peddle their elixirs and magic potions, London's literary project would highlight the materialistic base of all (supposed) metaphysics and dramatize the most elemental of pursuits in the unabating quest for the nutritive source of life itself. This quest-for-meat motif is especially evident in his most widely read writings – *The Call of the Wild*, *White Fang*, 'To Build a Fire' and

*The Sea-Wolf.* Imparting the thoughts of his wolf-dog protagonist in his 1906 novel *White Fang*, for example, he gets to the essence of the matter: 'The aim of life was meat. Life itself was meat. Life lived on life. There were the eaters and the eaten. The law was: EAT OR BE EATEN.'[19] London's writing typically excelled at describing reality in a way that was brutal but realistic.

As an adult, his writing, beefy as it so often was, would offer some degree of compensation for his early trauma, but his memories were distressing. His childhood, at least as he remembered it, was complicated by insecurity in terms of money and status, but also a confusion borne of a lack of affection from his mother. Though John London was gentle, and Jennie – along with his devoted stepsister Eliza – provided an important amount of emotional stability, he begrudged his mother's coldness. His feelings of scarcity became linked to his mother's aloofness as a parent. In a biography of her father, Joan London described her grandmother as a 'closemouthed woman'.[20] Although Flora was intelligent, self-reliant and active, outward displays of affection or warmth played little part in her personality when she was with London. Her impassive nature stung her son, who loved his mother dearly and from an early age (and as an adult) was distraught by the absence of a more keenly charged emotional connection with her. 'I do not remember', London claimed, 'ever receiving a caress from my mother when I was young.'[21] Though he had a tendency to exaggerate when recounting his early years, this statement suggests an element of truth.

Though Flora devoted herself to radical beliefs and embraced an alternative lifestyle, she had also become, in a more conventional sense, déclassée. Her socio-economic status had sunk well below the 'Wheat King' lifestyle of her youth. This socio-economic fall also seems to have fuelled a certain racial chauvinism, for she often reminded London that, unlike those of Greek or Italian descent, they were of old Anglo-American stock and that 'brunettes and all the tribe of dark-eyed humans were deceitful'.[22] Significantly, race would become an issue that he would return to again and again in his writings and that he would struggle with throughout his career – sometimes espousing racist views, while at other times advocating anti-racist and anti-colonial positions.

A strong desire to regain some social standing and economic status was behind Flora's frenetic but unsuccessful efforts to make money during London's formative years. With John London, their ventures included a partnership in a grocery store, raising chickens, storekeeping, overseeing a boarding house and farming, but they never prospered. London found the prospects of life in the cellar of society harrowing and would come to see that despite all the hype about upward mobility in America, those who were born in the working class almost always stayed in the working class. Nevertheless, he was determined to escape. Later in his adolescence he would take advantage of physical mobility – by land and sea – but his initial flights of freedom were those of the imagination.

The family relocated frequently during the first ten years of London's life. For his first three and a half years, they rented a series of residences in San Francisco. Then, after he and Eliza had barely survived a serious diphtheria epidemic, the family moved to Oakland, living at five different addresses from 1879 to 1881. The Londons next moved to Alameda, where John farmed on a 20-acre (8 ha) plot. At the age of five on the Alameda ranch, London had his first experience with alcohol. While John London was ploughing the field, he sent his son on a half-mile run to fetch a pail of beer. The open pail was filled to the brim and to prevent the beer from sloshing over the sides onto his legs, London decided to take a drink. After all, he had heard from the grown-ups that beer was good. 'Trust the grown-ups,' he reasoned, 'They knew.'[23] Though repelled by its taste, London gulped a sizeable quantity of the brew and stirred the remainder with a stick to cover the missing portion with foam. His unsuspecting father did not notice. He 'emptied the pail with the thirst of the sweating plowman' and resumed tilling.

Studio portrait of Jack London as a young boy with his dog, Rollo, *c.* 1885.

The sozzled little London attempted to follow beside the horses, but collapsed in a drunken stupor and was nearly disembowelled by the plough. With the world reeling in his inebriated state, he was carried by John to the edge of the field to recuperate under some trees. 'I was exhausted,' London recalled, 'oppressed by the weight of my limbs, and in my stomach was a harp-like vibration that extended to my throat and brain. My condition was like that of one who had gone through a battle with poison. In truth, I had been poisoned.' It would take a number of years, but he would eventually develop a 'sneaking liking' for alcohol.[24]

The family moved to a ranch in San Mateo County in 1883 and leased acreage to cultivate potatoes and raise horses. Later that year, they purchased a ranch in Livermore that had fruit orchards, vineyards, horses and chickens. The eight-year-old London was distraught when his beloved teenaged stepsister Eliza, who had been a font of emotional security for the boy, moved out to marry the 41-year-old Captain James Shepard. Though he had his adored dog Rollo, he was lonely in these countryside abodes, complaining that 'life on a California ranch was then to me the dullest existence possible'. Reading was the one activity that alleviated his boredom. 'I always could read and write,' he maintained, 'and have no recollection antedating such a condition. Folks say I simply insisted upon being taught.'[25] He was captivated by Paul du Chaillu's African travel narratives and Washington Irving's *Alhambra*. Ouida's novel *Signa*, which told the story of an Italian peasant boy's struggle to overcome poverty and achieve fame as a composer, was an especially significant influence. In a 1914 letter, he wrote that 'the story of Signa . . . put in me an ambition to get beyond the skylines of my narrow California valley and opened up to me the possibilities of the world of art. In fact it became my star to which I hitched my child's wagon.'[26] The novel's rags-to-riches paradigm, which he also encountered in reading the popular Horatio Alger books, was a model he would emulate in his own life, though his enormous literary and financial successes would be tempered by divorce, bouts of despair, alcoholism, health problems and various other misfortunes.

Living in the country during these years, he first began sensing a divide in his personality. He was starting to grapple with the complexity of his burgeoning artistic sensibility. 'I was a solitary and lonely child. Yet I was a social youngster, and always got along well with other children. I was healthy, hearty, normal and therefore happy, but I can see now that I lived a dual life. My outward life', he maintained, 'was that of the everyday poor man's son in the public school: rough and tumble, happy go lucky, jostled by a score, a hundred rough elements. Within myself I was reflective, contemplative, apart from the kinetic forces around me.'[27] The emerging intricacies of his inner life seemed at odds with the rustic realities of rural California. He remembered the Livermore ranch as 'squalid and sordid' and hated his chore-filled life that, he said, 'tended to drive me into myself and added to my inward powers of contemplation'.[28] The family moved back to Oakland from Livermore in 1886, after disease wiped out their brood of chickens. It was an especially unsteady period for the family. Their attempt to run a boarding house on East Seventeenth Street soon failed, and they moved a number of times during the next year. They finally ended up renting a house in a shoddier section of town on Pine Street in West Oakland from 1888 to 1890.

London began working to supplement the family income by selling newspapers on the Oakland streets. With morning and evening routes, he made about $3 a month. In addition, he worked various odd jobs, including setting up pins in a bowling alley, sweeping floors and working on an ice-delivery wagon. He also made a momentous find in his discovery of the Oakland Public Library. It became his happy refuge, his intellectual cache and his creative escape – a place where he could cultivate his interior imaginative richness. Furtively, he was sensitive, defiant and impassioned, while on the outside he appeared conventional, obedient and dutiful. Unbeknown to others, he was beginning to rebel and chafe against the inadequacies he encountered at home and to resist the bleakness he found on the Oakland streets where he sold his papers. He wrote to his editors at Houghton Mifflin in 1900 that 'from my ninth year with the exception of hours spent at school (and I earned them by hard labor), my life has been one of toil. It is worthless to give the long sordid list of occupations, none of them trades, all heavy manual labor.'[29] Yet he made time to read. His rapt incursion into the world of books reflected his questing urge to escape drudgery. In the Oakland library with its 'thousands of books', he recollected, 'I discovered all the great world beyond the skyline.' Luckily, Ina Coolbrith, a well-known literary figure in the Bay Area who was to become California's first poet laureate, was the librarian at the time. She noticed the boy's precocious reading habits and helped guide his book selections. 'It was this world of books now accessible,' he acknowledged, 'that practically gave me the basis of my education.'[30] He read novels by Melville, Stevenson, Kipling, Dickens and the voyages of Captain Cook. 'I read everything,' he later remarked, 'but principally history and adventure, and all the old travels and voyages. I read mornings, afternoons, and nights. I read in bed, I read at table, I read as I walked to and from school, and I read at recess while the other boys were playing.'[31] Though London's popular identity usually centres on the theatrical image of a rugged adventurer, he became a discerning, sensitive, constant and wide-ranging reader – part perspicacious aesthete and part rational intellectual – who was well versed in mythology, science and evolution, politics, history, philosophy, psychology and the Bible. Notably, the genesis of much of London's creative output emerges from a fertile opposition between the dynamic qualities of his feverish imagination and the gritty, real-world naturalistic focus for which so much of his work is renowned. That is, although he wanted to write truthfully about life on the guts-and-meat level, he also found himself driven by visions and ideas that he had difficulty reducing to biological causes.

Around this time, London also enrolled at the Cole Grammar School, where he met his lifelong friend Frank Atherton. In his memoir *Jack London in Boyhood Adventures*, Atherton recalls that during recess at Cole, while the other children engaged in various playground antics and games, London would retire to a wooden bench to read on his own. One day the school bully, Mike Panell, confronted London on the playground: 'Hey, kid, why doncha ever play wid us guys? Doncha get enough of books in da schoolroom, widout readin' at recess like a sissy? . . . Think yer somebody, better'n us guys, sneaking off by yerself ta read a crazy ol' book? Yuh better git on to yerself an git yer mug outta that book, an be a sport like us guys.'[32] London tried to ignore him and continued reading, but Mike snatched the book from him and threw it in the dirt. He sprang at Mike, punching him in the nose and knocking him to the ground. A crowd gathered around the two, chanting 'Fight! Fight!' Mike pulled a knife, but he was disarmed by some of the onlookers and the two were sent to the principal's office. The principal offered to suspend their punishment if they would hug and make up. Mike was willing but London refused. "'I'll take the licking," he told the principal, "I know I was in the right, and I'd do it again if I have to defend myself."' The incident made London into something of a hero to his classmates, one of whom remarked, 'Gosh, Johnny, I didn't know you could fight like that. You must've taken boxing lessons, I'll bet Mike won't tackle you again. He's just a dirty coward, anyway.'[33] Atherton and London soon became fast friends, and when London was not working or reading, the two hunted mud hens, ducks and wildcats with their slingshots, explored Chinatown, went boating, and attended plays and operas at local theatres.

On one of their escapades, London and Frank set out to hunt birds on the stark wilds of the Alameda marsh, accompanied by London's dog, a collie-shepherd mix and devoted companion.

When London slightly wounded a heron with his slingshot, Shep suddenly went berserk and bolted across the marsh yelping crazily. They pursued her, but 'on she ran, first in one direction, then in another . . . getting further away from us. Yet we ran on and on, heedless of our own danger of falling into the deep mudholes that prevailed in every direction.'[34] Shep abruptly disappeared, swallowed up in the quagmire of one of the mudholes. After a frantic search, they found the beloved pup floundering in 'the slimy muck, struggling in the last throes of death'. Miraculously, the boys were able to drag Shep out of the oozy pit to safety. The sludge had nearly suffocated the dog, and though she was utterly exhausted, Shep recovered. "'I'll never take her to that damned old marsh again," he rued. "I should have known better. What a fool I was."'[35]

Atherton also recounts visiting the London household while Flora was conducting one of her seances. London was sitting alone on the porch. Frank could hear muffled voices and strange moans emanating from within. Sheepishly, London began to explain to his friend that his mother was 'a spiritualist medium', who met with her followers to communicate with 'manifestations of departed persons'.[36] He went on to explain to Frank that Flora contacted the dead through the spirit Indian Chief known as Plume. London found these gatherings comedic and foolish, declaring to Frank, 'I don't believe in spirits and ghosts . . . It's all nonsense. When a person dies, that's the end so far as he is concerned.'[37] His early uneasiness with his mother's spiritualism probably stimulated London towards espousing materialist and atheistic views later in life, but notable traces of the supernatural often lurk beneath and around his avowed naturalistic orientation.

In the summer of 1889, he was granted a welcome reprieve from his part-time jobs when his parents allowed him to enjoy an extended holiday with Frank's family in idyllic Auburn, a former California gold rush town near Sacramento. Here the boys roved over mountains, explored the wooded glens and swam in rivers.

It was the first time London had had the leisure to fully immerse himself in the natural landscape and enjoy the pastoral countryside of California. In the autumn, though, it was back to work and to Cole Grammar School. He often sailed on the Bay in a small boat he had purchased for $2 and refurbished.[38] On the tricky coastal waters, he was developing vital boating skills and becoming a dexterous sailor. Recalling his youthful nautical adventures in his essay 'The Joy of Small-boat Sailing', he wrote that compared to motor boating, sailing requires 'more skill, more intelligence, and a vast deal more training [and] is the finest training in the world for boy and youth and man. If the boy is very small, equip him with a small, comfortable skiff. He will do the rest. He won't need to be taught.'[39] In 1890 London was finishing what was to be his final full year of formal schooling. The family needed the extra income, and his next destination would be the factory.

Certainly, his early years were trying and precarious, but they were not wretched. And, to be fair, Flora's industrious devotion to financial survival did, if barely, keep the family afloat. John London was a willing partner in their endeavours, but his health issues increasingly hampered his physical capacities and rendered him something of a liability in the rough and tumble capitalist scramble of California. London's negative recollections are clearly bound up with his mother's thwarted ambitions and gnawing sense of displacement – few things are more wearisome than being downwardly mobile in America. Scholars generally agree that London somewhat embellished the poverty and hardship of his childhood, and these tendencies can be informative because they reveal a psyche that was sensitive but driven. The privations of his early years aggravated his creative spirit and spurred his ambition and desire for adventure. London's hypersensitivity to the trials of his youth are inextricable from, and balanced by, his compensatory striving character. 'As I see it,' wrote his second wife, Charmian Kittredge London, 'his excessive sensibilities, despite formidable endurance, caused him to suffer more acutely, mentally and physically, than the average run of human beings. Since his increasing ambitions to do and be, goaded him ever to superactivity, his case was hopeless, in that he must undergo weariness of heart and brain.' She adds, 'he could not rest, therefore he did not rest. Hence, I occasionally found him prone to exaggerate, not the thing in itself, but the enormity of the thing treated.'[40] His early limitations exasperated but also motivated the young writer. If he groused disproportionately about his ill fortune, he strove exceedingly for remedies. London always wanted something better, something new, something different. He always wanted more and ceaselessly looked beyond and above for more love, more excitement, more adventure, more knowledge, more answers, more equity and more justice.

While he was much pained by the monotonous toil and grubbing poverty of a working-class life, these same circumstances stoked his aspirations to travel and find adventure in exotic faraway places. He knew he wanted to escape the grinding rut of his working-class prospects. Still, he always identified with the workers and deplored how the less fortunate were exploited, abused and stereotyped. In speeches, essays and fiction, he would regularly esteem and defend their energy and generosity and solidarity. Though the proletariat could be loutish, they were remarkably generous, authentic and resourceful. He also soon discovered that the lower classes were liberally peppered with sophisticated and original thinkers. To his dismay, he would find that many in the privileged echelons of society were glib, ignorant, selfish and incompetent. An inveterate synthesizer of divergent philosophies and alternating modes of being, he wanted to retain the dynamism of his working-class origins and – as soon as possible – partake of the cultural refinements and heady adventures that lay beyond the confines of his hardscrabble youth.

# 2

# Desperado: Wharf Rat, Oyster Pirate, Road Kid (1889–92)

Better to reign among booze-fighters, a prince, than to toil twelve hours a day at a machine for ten cents an hour.
Jack London[1]

Ours the wild life in tumult still to range
From toil to rest, and joy in every change.
Lord Byron[2]

When London graduated from Cole Grammar School in 1889 he refused to attend the graduation ceremony because his family could not afford to buy him a proper suit. The reality was that his parents urgently needed his financial support. He would have to continue with his paper route and odd jobs until he could find employment at a factory. This meant forgoing any additional education or apprenticeship to learn a trade. He spent what little free time he had sailing a small skiff in the Bay and began prowling deeper into the seedy netherworld around the Oakland waterfront and San Francisco docks. He was fascinated by the old salts, ex-cons and raiders who populated the local wharves and saloons. For him, these raffish seadogs beckoned a call to the realm of exciting nautical adventures beyond the chronic poverty of his youth.

By the age of fourteen, he was honing his boating skills sailing his spindly 4-metre (14 ft) decked-over skiff on the Oakland estuary and sometimes even out into the more perilous waters of San Francisco Bay. 'I was in the flower of my adolescence,' he recalled, 'a-thrill with romance and adventure, dreaming of a wild life in the wild man-world.'[3] One day, while preparing to launch his skiff, he met a seventeen-year-old lad named Scotty, who claimed to be a runaway apprentice and sailor. He was looking for a berth on a whaling ship and asked if London would ferry him out to the *Idler*, a big sloop-yacht anchored in the estuary. Scotty wanted to meet up with the boat's caretaker, a nineteen-year-old harpooner who was getting ready to ship out on a whaler. London was thrilled at the chance to see the *Idler* up close. Having heard rumours that the *Idler* was an opium-smuggling vessel out of the Sandwich Islands, he had been admiring the yacht at a 'wistful distance' for some time.[4] Once aboard, he was dazzled by the ship's rough-hewn nautical interior with its musty sea gear – sou'westers, sea-boots and oilskins: 'At last I was living. Here I sat inside my first ship, a smuggler, accepted as a comrade by a harpooner and a runway English sailor.'[5] They drank rotgut out of tumblers and London listened intently as the two young mariners spun seafaring yarns about rounding the Cape, Arctic voyages and North Pacific gales. 'Drink was the badge of manhood,' and as the alcohol flowed, London became less reticent and bragged of the time he crossed San Francisco Bay in a howling storm – asserting that he was the best small-boat sailor of the now thoroughly inebriated trio.[6] Scotty took offence, but they had another round, made up, pledged everlasting friendship, drank more and belted out a mishmash of sea shanties.

In his 1913 confessional memoir *John Barleycorn*, this reminiscence marks the first major instance in his life when drink becomes personified as 'John Barleycorn', a ghostly figure London calls his 'adopted twin brother and *alter ego*'.[7] From this point on in his life, John Barleycorn would be a most curious companion –

George Fiske, *Sunset Study, San Francisco Bay*, 1884, photograph.

a welcome enabler for male camaraderie and general bonhomie, but also a catalyst for disillusion and depression. Alcohol could exhilarate and liberate – but only for a time. Inevitably, heavy drinking peeled away convenient delusions and exposed the bald pessimism of a despairing nihilism he called the 'white logic'. But for now, he and his friends were being spirited upward by their bounteous swill. 'We were not ordinary. We were three tipsy young gods, incredibly wise, gloriously genial, and without limit to our powers. Ah! – and I say it now, after the years – could John Barleycorn keep one at such a height, I should never draw a sober breath again.'[8] He was soon to discover that John Barleycorn exacted excruciating tolls. 'One pays,' as he explained, 'according to an iron schedule – for every strength the balanced weakness; for every high a corresponding low; for every fictitious god-like moment an equivalent time in reptilian slime.'[9]

With John Barleycorn 'tricking [his] fancy' London finally felt as if he was not merely reading about adventure but actually living it.[10] In this bacchanal he had, it seemed, at long last transcended the mundane: 'I was beginning to grasp the meaning of life. Here was no commonplace, no Oakland Estuary, no weary round of throwing newspapers at front doors, delivering ice, and setting up ninepins. All the world was mine.'[11] They continued drinking, ascending to the heights of exaltation with John Barleycorn, but soon Scotty's coordination began to break down and he passed out cold in his bunk. Soon thereafter the harpooner faded into his own somnolent oblivion, and London 'was left alone, unthrown, on the field of battle'.[12]

Still inspired by Bacchus and eager to test his manhood, he debarked from the *Idler* and steered his frail skiff into a 65-kilometre-per-hour (40 mph) wind. As he sang 'Blow the Man Down', the boat plunged through the raging surf: 'I was no boy

Harvey Thomas Dunn, 'I was a man, a god', illustration in Jack London's *John Barleycorn* (1913).

of fourteen, living the mediocre ways of the sleepy town called Oakland. I was a man, a god, and the very elements rendered me allegiance as I bitted them to my will.'[13] But it was low tide, and when he sailed back to the wharf he had to drag his boat across a hundred-yard mud bank to get back to the docks. It was at this point that the alcohol took full effect. Suddenly, London's own coordination broke down, and he tumbled into the muddy slime, deeply scraping his arms on sharp, bacteria-laced barnacles. He was hung-over for two days and could barely move his infected arms for a week. Never again, he vowed, but the night had been unlike anything he had experienced before. It was a 'purple passage flung into the monotony of [his] days'.[14] This revelatory drama proved to him that he was indeed fit for a life at sea; furthermore, the experience offered eminently valuable material for the future writer, as it granted a rare insight into human behaviour: 'I had got behind men's souls. I had got behind my own soul and found unguessed potencies and greatnesses.'[15]

In her biography of her husband, Charmian Kittredge London singles out this night as a demarcation point, the crucial threshold where the author's childhood ended and his life 'became indissolubly bound with the affairs of men'.[16] Alcohol as an anodyne had much to do with the opening up of a wider (and more treacherous) world for London. When he had visited saloons with his father a few years earlier, he had sensed something exceptional in those exclusively male settings. Even back then, the pulsating fellowship and spectacle of the saloon world stood in sharp contrast to his otherwise grubby, labour-filled life. Saloons were portals out of the menial grind where, as London attested,

> life was different. Men talked with great voices, laughed with great laughs, and there was always an atmosphere of greatness. Here was something more than common every-day where nothing happened. Here life was always very live, and,

sometimes, even lurid, when blows were struck and blood was shed, and big policemen came shouldering in. Great moments, these, for me, my head filled with all the wild and valiant fighting of the gallant adventures on sea and land.[17]

Saloons were places of excitement and wonder that stirred London's striving character to know 'that something beyond, which [he] sensed and groped after'.[18] 'There were no big moments,' said London, 'when I trudged along the street throwing my papers in at doors. But in the saloons, even the sots, stupefied, sprawling across the tables or in the sawdust, were objects of mystery and wonder.'[19]

By age fifteen he claimed he could easily hold his own drinking with grown men, and his boyish spirit, good humour and sharp intelligence must have been a lively tonic to the crusty band of mariners and ne'er-do-wells of the waterfront. While most of the nation's young literati were living sheltered lives and plodding through the rote instruction of high school, London was rubbing shoulders with some of the more twisted and rascally specimens of humanity. Could a future writer ask for better material?

It was sometime after his experience on the *Idler* that London went to work full time in a factory. Exact dates during this period of his life are difficult to pin down, but at some point in the autumn of 1889 or early winter of 1890, London started his job at Hickmott's Cannery in West Oakland. The building had been converted from an old horse stable into a canning factory and the working conditions were appalling. For 10 cents an hour, he soldered cans and stuffed pickles into jars – and he worked alongside children as young as six and seven. Workers could quit, but economic conditions were such that owners could easily restaff from a plentiful surplus labour market. Often toiling for twelve or fourteen hours a day, he would go to and from work never seeing the light of day. 'Many a night,' he recounted,

I did not knock off work until midnight. On occasion I worked
eighteen and twenty hours on a stretch. Once I worked at
my machine for thirty-six consecutive hours. And there were
weeks on end when I never knocked off work earlier than
eleven o'clock, got home and in bed at half after midnight,
and was called at half-past five to dress, eat, walk to work,
and be at my machine at seven o'clock whistle blow.[20]

One of London's finest stories, 'The Apostate', draws on his
experiences as a child labourer. Written in 1906 for magazine
publication, it delivers a powerful denunciation of exploitative
working conditions that alienate individuals and divide families.
An overriding sense of pathos governs the story's depiction of
Johnny, a boy who has worked as a factory labourer from the age
of seven. 'He was', London writes, 'the perfect worker. He knew
that. He had been told so, often . . . From the perfect worker he had
evolved into the perfect machine.'[21] The factory is a proletarian
Hades where workers are subjected to the dictates of free-market
production. Its demands are relentless, mechanized and numbing.
Working conditions transform organic, feeling, sentient human
beings into anaesthetized automatons. Unrelenting efficiency
squelches compassion and automation blots out consciousness.
The resulting commodification of self – a metamorphosis into pure
mechanism – is at the gruesome core of the narrative:

> There was no joyousness in life for [Johnny]. The
> procession of the days he never saw. The nights he slept
> away in twitching unconsciousness. The rest of the
> time he worked, and his consciousness was machine
> consciousness. Outside this his mind was a blank . . .
> He was a work-beast. He had no mental life whatever.[22]

The governing motif of the story is darkness. Johnny wakes in darkness, enters the factory in darkness, toils at his machine for hours and returns home in darkness – the benighted existence of a wage slave. But the virtuosity of London's story lies in his grim depiction of the deplorable living and working conditions Johnny and his family are forced to endure. His desperate single-parent mother must use Johnny's wages to help support the younger children in the family and to give his younger brother Will the opportunity to become a bookkeeper to help alleviate their penury. For Johnny, the deprivation is a form of spiritual and bodily vampirism. London writes that Will 'was well-built, fairly rugged, as tall as his elder brother and even heavier. It was as though the life-blood of the one had been diverted into the other's veins. And in spirits it was the same, Johnny was jaded, worn out, without resilience, while his younger brother seemed bursting and spilling over with exuberance.'[23] In the end, Johnny chooses his only escape route: he abandons family and factory, hits the road and becomes a hobo. His decision signifies the shedding of his working-class false consciousness: the repudiation of his devotion to the work ethic – the apostasy of the story's title. His decision is more of a lateral move than a triumph, and though he may be escaping the industrial maw, nothing is resolved for those he leaves behind. In Johnny's absence, his younger brother Will is the next in line to support the family, and now he will go on to suffer the brutal factory conditions. The inexorable cycle of working-class economic immobility continues. Recalling his own bleak time in the cannery, London queried, 'I asked myself if this were the meaning of life – to be a work-beast? I knew of no horse in the city of Oakland that worked the hours I worked. If this were living, I was entirely unenamoured of it.'[24] London's own escape route was at least as risky as Johnny's. To escape working-class wage slavery, he wilfully descended into the shadowy world of the Oakland waterfront.

While still toiling away at the cannery, London got word that a waterfront acquaintance named French Frank was selling his sailing boat the *Razzle Dazzle* for $300. French Frank was a seasoned 'oyster pirate', one of the local poachers who raided corporate-owned oyster beds in the Bay and slyly sold their tasty plunder along the city wharves to restaurant owners and saloon keepers. Most of the beds they raided were owned by the Southern Pacific Railroad, a massive conglomerate distained by the locals. The beds were guarded by armed patrolmen, so the pillaging was not only a felony but a potentially lethal enterprise. Due to the unpopularity of Southern Pacific, however, authorities tended to turn a blind eye to oyster buccaneering. City police, in fact, were often first in line to sample the oyster pirate's delicacies on the wharves. Though its price tag was high, London saw the *Razzle Dazzle* as his ticket out of the factory and onto the water. He could be an independent freebooter at last! 'I wanted to be where the winds of adventure blew,' he mused. 'And the winds of adventure blew the oyster pirate ships up and down San Francisco Bay.'[25] He had read enough about adventure; now he was ready to live it on a regular basis. With his pluck and knack for sailing he could make as much money raiding oyster beds in a night or two than he could slogging away for a month in the cannery. Luckily, he was able to borrow the $300 from his foster mother Jennie Prentiss, who was gainfully employed as a nurse. After arranging the sale with French Frank, they sealed the deal with friends and a prodigious jug of wine, frolicking into the night aboard the new vessel London himself would soon command. French Frank's paramour Mamie (known locally as the Queen of the Oyster Pirates) was in attendance and clearly had eyes for the handsome young sailor. At first, the romantically naive London was oblivious to her overtures, but, as legend has it, she eventually managed to make her interests unmistakably palpable. Such was the pirate's life, and London adapted willingly. He soon became known among his cronies as the Prince of the Oyster Pirates.

For the next eighteen months or so, he wholly embraced the sordid but invigorating piratical life. He drank hard and often, proved a gutsy oyster raider, had several close calls with the authorities and survived many a feisty clash with assorted ruffians. His scruffy entourage included toughs with names like Old Smoudge, Whiskey Bob, Joe Goose, Spider Healey and Clam. Another notorious companion, Captain Nelson, was known as Old Scratch, and his son, accordingly, went by the moniker Young Scratch. Old Scratch got his name 'from a Berserker trick of his, in fighting, of tearing off his opponent's face'.[26] London also made a substantial amount of money looting oysters and succeeded in paying back his loan from Jennie Prentiss and providing regular financial support for his mother and father. For the first time in his life, he had ample surplus income. Achieving what he termed a 'trans-valuing of values', he soon learned to leave behind his working-class thriftiness and embrace the carefree spending habits of the waterfront saloon crowd.[27]

In this new environment, spending was more advantageous (and more fun) than the working-class virtues of scrimping and saving. Initially, this new lavishness was a difficult practice to accept for someone used to toiling for 10 cents an hour and conditioned by a life of scarcity, but this new concept was driven home one night when he was drinking with Young Scratch Nelson at Johnny Heinold's First and Last Chance Saloon, one of London's hangouts of choice. On this night, London was delighted to be drinking with Nelson, who was a renowned Bay adventurer. With veteran waterfront largesse, Nelson treated London to a beer as they chatted about boats and swiping oysters. London was disinclined to drink beer, despising the taste, but noted that 'Nelson had a strange quirk of nature that made him find happiness in treating me to beer.' But, he reasoned, 'just because I didn't like the taste of it and the weight of it was no reason I should forgo the honor of his company.'[28] Hobnobbing at the bar that evening, Nelson treated him to six beers. After leaving the saloon, London felt a vague uneasiness with regard to Nelson's unstinting generosity. Then, out of some remote region of his consciousness, he recollected the boyhood code about sharing candy: 'When on a day a fellow gave another a "cannon-ball" or a chunk of taffy, on some other day he would expect to receive back a cannon-ball or a chunk of taffy.'[29] Finally, he realized his moronic social gaffe at the saloon of not reciprocating in kind. What a blockhead he had been in front of the great Nelson! Recalling his embarrassment, he later wrote: 'I think, now, when I look back upon it, that Nelson was curious. He wanted to find out just what kind of a gink I was. He wanted to see how many times I'd let him treat without offering to treat in return.'[30] He now saw how frugality among the pirates was a colossal lapse in etiquette. Thrift was no longer a virtue. Freely spending money in this milieu was not as irresponsible as it would be for the factory worker; rather, the seeming excess of the waterfront was a means of establishing equity, ensuring sociability, developing solidarity. With the tit-for-tat custom of the waterfront, the more you spent, the more you got, and – most importantly – the more allies you acquired. 'Money no longer counted,' he finally understood. 'It was comradeship that counted.'[31] Buying a 10-cent beer for a 'gloomy, grouchy individual, who threatened to become an enemy, [made him] into a good friend, even genial, his looks were kindly, and our voices mellowed together as we talked water-front and oyster-bed gossip'.[32] Perhaps because London presents this scene somewhat drolly in *John Barleycorn*, readers tend to overlook the significance of the Nelson-six-beer episode, but it cogently encapsulates a thematic cornerstone in his fiction and in his life – the importance of reciprocity, which is the basis of comradeship. Reciprocity, interdependence and altruism are especially fundamental leitmotifs in London's Northland fiction, where survival depends not on individualism but on prosocial cooperative behaviour. Later on, such principles would readily dovetail with his more complexly conceived revolutionary socialist ideals. In his late teens, he became more and more disturbed by the socio-economic inequities of capitalism and by the predatory, competitive selfishness that he believed the market economy endorsed. Socialism, he believed, could ameliorate various social ills – especially with regard to workers' rights, poverty and income inequality.

For now, however, he operated contentedly on the shifty fringes of capitalist society and was quick to offer rationalizations for his criminal activities, maintaining that pirating was his way of avoiding an exploitative system. Consorting with deckhands, poachers and scroungers in his mid-teens also made him more cynical and hardened. His childhood friend Frank Atherton noted the alteration in London's demeanour around this time: 'He talked and acted like a far different lad – one who had abandoned all the grand ideals of his boyhood dreams and given himself up to the desperate life of an outlaw.'[33] Frank also reported that when he questioned his friend about his illegal raiding, London replied defensively, 'I admit it's risky, but life is made up of chances. And it beats working in those damned old sweatshops for starvation wages. Besides, I'm my own boss. There's nobody around to pound me on the back and yell at me to hurry.'[34] Frank pressed him further, questioning his cavalier disregard of moral principle and the possibility of getting arrested, and London riposted, 'What about the principle of the big corporations in keeping the poor working people ground down to ten cents an hour, while they themselves are piling up profits by the millions? They're robbing the workers of their right to live and depriving them of the bare necessities of life.'[35] His logic here may not have been exactly airtight, but, as usual, he was committed to defending his viewpoint and his actions.

London dramatized this rollicking and precarious time in his life in a 1902 novel he wrote for the young-adult market, *The Cruise of the Dazzler*. In the book, Joe Bronson, a privileged 'Hill-dweller' in San Francisco, decides that he has had enough of school and his soft 'sissy' acquaintances.[36] In search of a more authentic and daring life, he teams up with French Pete and the young 'Frisco Kid on a sloop called

Milton James Burns, 'Pete clung on, working inboard every time he emerged, till he dropped into the cockpit', frontispiece to Jack London's *The Cruise of the Dazzler* (1902).

the *Dazzler*. Captain Pete turns out to be a drunk, and Joe quickly finds that, with the exception of the good-hearted 'Frisco Kid, the waterfront 'adventurers' who seemed so romantic from a distance are actually abusive and knavish thieves. During the book's climactic getaway scene in Chapter Twenty, a notorious oyster pirate named Red Nelson steers his sleek sloop, the *Reindeer*, through a raging storm. As the water scuds across 'her decks in foaming cataracts' and the air is 'filled with flying spray', from the deck of the *Dazzler* Joe perceives Red Nelson in all his flawed, defiant glory at the helm of the *Reindeer*:

Red Nelson, his sou'wester gone and his fair hair plastered in wet, wind-blown ringlets about his face. His whole attitude breathed indomitability, courage, strength. It seemed almost as though the divine were blazing forth from him. Joe looked upon him in sudden awe, and, realizing the enormous possibilities of the man, felt sorrow for the way in which they had been wasted. A thief and a robber! In that flashing moment Joe caught a glimpse of human truth, grasped at the mystery of success and failure. Life threw back its curtains that he might read it and understand. Of such stuff as Red Nelson were heroes made; but they possessed wherein he lacked – the power of choice, the careful poise of mind, the sober control of soul: in short, the very things his father had so often 'preached' to him about.[37]

Seconds later, the *Reindeer* is engulfed by an immense wave and goes down with no survivors. Sensational as it is, the scene offers an early example of themes prevalent in London's fiction – corrupted potential, the limitations of free will, the power of nature and the revelation of character in moments of crisis. Though fitting for its juvenile audience, the novel's plot is pedestrian, its tone is moralistic and its characters are one-dimensional. London does, however, depict several vividly rendered passages on sailing and nautical manoeuvres on San Francisco Bay.

He enjoyed continued success raiding oyster beds, until a fire destroyed the *Razzle Dazzle*'s mainsail and soon after, rival miscreants pillaged the boat. He decided to join up with Young Scratch Nelson, and they prowled the Bay together in his sloop. But London was beginning to get pirate fatigue. The limitations of Bay life were growing more apparent. Despite a solid partnership with Nelson that was full of camaraderie and carousing, most of his fellow marauders were little more than cut-throat, small-time crooks. It was a dead-end racket. London knew most of them would shortly end up in prison or dead. He needed to get out while he still could.

Then, early in 1892, of all things, he claims to have teamed up with the Fish Patrol. A forerunner of the California Department of Fish and Wildlife, the Fish Patrol enforced regulations implemented to prevent overfishing and poaching. His name was never listed on the department's deputy directory, but the Fish Patrol may have used insiders like London in 'off-the-record' capacities to help track down and apprehend suspects.[38] To avoid run-ins with his old confederates, London moved to Benicia, about 65 kilometres (40 mi.) by boat to the northeast. He apparently had no real qualms about switching over to the side of the law, if indeed that was the case. He was the central character in the adventure story of his life and relocating in Benicia offered a fresh orientation.

A fictionalized version of his time with the Fish Patrol is presented in his 1905 collection *Tales of the Fish Patrol*. First published in the magazine *Youth's Companion*, and, like *The Cruise of the Dazzler*, written specifically for an adolescent audience, this work is noteworthy as a coherent example of the short-story cycle format – a series of linked or interrelated stories published in a single volume. He had used the short-story cycle form masterfully in his arrangement of the 1902 collection *Children of the Frost*, and also in two later books published in 1912, *Smoke Bellew* and *The Son of the Sun*. The *Fish Patrol* stories also show London depicting fishermen from different ethnic communities on San Francisco Bay – Chinese, Italian and Greek. His portrayal of non-white characters is sometimes sympathetic and nuanced, but at other times stereotypical and racist – a contradictory pattern that persisted throughout his career.

His time in Benicia provided a new and somewhat less hazardous means for London to preserve his independence, while allowing him to stay on the water and keep his distance from the factory. His partying and drinking, however, actually intensified. He found that 'good guys' guzzled alcohol just as much as (if not more than) 'bad guys'. It took little effort to find a 'congenial crowd of drinkers and vagabonds' on the Benicia docks with whom he could get sloshed on a regular basis.[39] One morning, he woke up on the dock to find his arms and legs ludicrously entangled in a fishing net he had drunkenly staggered into just before passing out after a hardy night of boozing. Royally plastered on another evening, he toppled into the water from a sloop and was swept away in the swift current that ran through the Carquinez Strait. The sozzled teenager willingly let his body float out with the tide, morosely entertaining thoughts of suicide. John Barleycorn, London later wrote, 'had played me his maniacal trick', making suicide by drowning seem 'fine, a splendid culmination, a perfect rounding off of my short but splendid career'.[40] Eventually, he sobered up and regained his will to live, but he spent four hours in the chilly water before being fortuitously rescued by a passing Greek fisherman.

Late in the summer of 1892, London returned to Oakland. For a $10 reward, he sailed up the Bay to retrieve a friend's stolen boat at Port Costa with his friend Nickey the Greek. They recovered the boat, but only after narrowly escaping an irate dock constable. To evade the authorities, the best getaway route was to sail north and lie low for a spell in Sacramento. Near Sacramento, he encountered a gaggle of 'road kids' swimming on a sand bar near a railroad bridge. Nickey and London fell in with the group. This band of ragamuffins was an intriguing new breed of vagabond. He was fascinated by their slang and the tales they told of inland journeys over the Sierra Nevada mountains and beyond. Mostly homeless runaways, they criss-crossed the country, hopping trains, tramping, panhandling. 'These wanderers made my oyster-piracy look like thirty cents,' he thought. 'A new world was calling to me in every word that was spoken – a world of rods and gunnels, blind baggages and "side-door Pullmans," "bulls" and "shacks," "floppings" and "chewin's," "pinches" and "get-aways," "strong arms" and "bindle-stiffs," "punks" and "profesh." And it all spelled Adventure.'[41] Nickey returned to Oakland, but London stayed on with the road kids. As always, he was game for new adventures and fresh challenges. 'I "lined" myself up alongside those road-kids. I was just as strong as any of them, just as quick, just as nervy, and my brain was just as good.'[42] That summer he managed to hop an eastbound train out of Sacramento and ride it 'over the hill', crossing the Sierra Nevada and back to Sacramento. This feat officially granted him admittance to join the 'push', or gang, as a 'full-fledged road-kid'.[43] They called him Sailor Kid, and later he was known as the 'Frisco Kid. He possessed the physical agility and street smarts to acclimatize himself to the rigours of road life, but he had to overcome reservations regarding the accepted road-kid practice of street begging. From his oyster-pirating days he had internalized the notion that stealing was morally superior to begging, and 'that robbery was finer still because the risk and penalty were proportionately greater'. For London, to 'rob was manly; to beg was sordid and despicable'.[44] Necessity, though, became the agent of another 'trans-valuing of values' for the rookie tramp. Broke, hungry and not wanting to mooch off other road kids, he expediently came to see begging as 'a joyous prank, a game, a nerve exerciser'.[45] He recounts much of his road-kid life in his 1907 memoir, *The Road*, where he describes train-hopping methods, crafty techniques for eluding the railroad 'bulls' (watchmen) and how packs of road kids stalked and 'rolled' (mugged) unwary drunks.

Later that autumn, he was ready to take a break from tramping and made his way back to Oakland. He refrained from oyster-pirating and worked various odd jobs to get by. He did resume sousing it up mightily in the local saloons with Nelson and company. 'I became pretty thoroughly alcohol soaked during this period,' he later admitted. 'I practically lived in saloons; became a bar-room loafer, and worse.'[46] During an election parade rally, he got monstrously smashed drinking straight whisky, instigated a brawl on a train and nearly died of alcohol poisoning. The near-fatal episode prompted him to see 'the death-road which John Barleycorn maintains for his devotees'.[47] The refrain he heard from old friends now in prison was: 'If I hadn't been drunk I wouldn't a done it.'[48] He also noticed that habitual drinkers tended to perish readily in freakish accidents and from minor illnesses. 'I was getting into a bad way of living,' he acknowledged. The drinking life 'made toward death too quickly to suit my youth and my vitality'.[49] He drank more cautiously, but was on the lookout for a way to make a decisive break from the waterfront.

# 3

# Young Adventurer: Pacific Sailor and American Tramp (1893–4)

Oh, it was raw, believe me; but the life we lived was raw, and we were as raw as the life.

Jack London[1]

Where Jack London differed most essentially from his rough-neck associates was in the divine unrest that forever withheld him from content with any static condition. One thing or a group of things mastered, he was done with it so far as it represented an end, and hot on the trail of the unexplored.

Charmian Kittredge London[2]

During the winter of 1892 a battery of Pacific sealing ships was anchored in San Francisco Bay for repair and provisioning. Their layover gave London the chance to fraternize with crew members from various sealers in waterfront saloons, and he was captivated by their adventurous yarns. Blue-water sailing across the Pacific was an enticing new horizon and he could not resist this alluring call: 'It was curiosity, desire to know, an unrest and a seeking for things wonderful. . . . What was this life for, I demanded, if this were all? No; there was something more, away and beyond.'[3] London hit it off with a young seal hunter named Pete Holt and agreed to accompany Holt as a boat puller on his next voyage. On 20 January 1893, eight days after his seventeenth birthday, London signed on as crew member of the schooner *Sophia Sutherland* bound for Japan and the far northwest of the Pacific Ocean. It was a bold move for the teenage small-boat sailor, who had barely ventured beyond the Golden Gate. But this was his first chance to finally embark on the adventurous path into that great beyond that he had been dreaming and reading about for years. With his typical bravado, he signed on as an able-bodied seaman, a rank usually requiring three years of deep-water sailing experience and a minimum age of nineteen. He probably slipped by with some crafty guidance from Pete Holt and thanks to his own already ingrained maritime swagger. At a lean 73 kilograms (160 lb), London stood at only 1.7 metres (5 ft 7 in.), but had broad, powerful shoulders and muscular arms and legs. Though still youthful, his rugged demeanour undeniably 'smacked' of the sea.

He realized, however, that special measures would be necessary to adapt himself to the bigger ship, its veteran crew and the trans-Pacific passage. This deep-water voyage aboard the three-masted sealer would obviously require a different set of seafaring skills. It also would be a challenge to gain the acceptance of his fellow shipmates aboard the *Sophia Sutherland*. They were mainly hard-bitten old tars of Scandinavian stock. And, unlike London, most had worked their way up through the rigid maritime hierarchy to become able-bodied seamen from the lowly positions of cooks, cabin boys and ordinary seamen. In the process they had endured severe and often downright cruel treatment from senior shipmates. London was aware that his mates would inevitably resent the youngster's seemingly free ascent to an equal rank. He needed to learn the names and uses of all the new lines and riggings, but he was up to the task: 'I *was* an able seaman . . . I had graduated from the right school. As a small-boat sailor I had learned to reason out and know the *why* of everything.'[4]

The other sailors knew that this was the fresh-faced newbie's first oceanic voyage, and London knew it was imperative to prove

E. L. Weule, *Sophia Sutherland in a Drydock*, undated photograph.

his sailing talents and physical toughness straightaway. Because of his youth and inexperience, he set out to be extra-industrious to maintain his equal standing with the other eleven men in the forecastle. 'I resolved to do my work, no matter how hard or dangerous it might be, so well that no man would be called upon to do it for me. Further, I put ginger in my muscles. I never malingered when pulling on a rope, for I know the eagle eyes of my forecastle mates were squinting for just such evidence of my inferiority.'[5] He was always the first of the watch on deck, made sure to leave no ropes uncoiled and never hesitated to climb aloft to shift or set the topsails. To ensure camaraderie and to pay his dues as a neophyte, he consistently did more than his share to stave off any ill will.

All went well on the outward voyage until he had a run-in with a cranky Swede named Big Red John, a behemoth of a sailor who thought he could bully the much smaller and younger London. Each seaman had what was called a 'Peggy day' on which it was his assigned duty to clean the forecastle and do scullery work. On Big Red John's 'Peggy day' he gruffly ordered London, who was busy weaving a rope-yarn mat, to refill a condiment jar of molasses. To Big Red John's and everyone else's astonishment, London curtly refused to do the giant seaman's bidding. When the big Swede smacked him in the face for his impudence, London whipped around and punched him right between the eyes. The kid's audacity shocked the other sailors. They thought London was about to get the bilge pounded out of him for sure. But in a flash, he somehow scrambled onto Big Red John's upper back and got a firm hold on his throat – choking him and viciously clawing away at his windpipe. Unable to dislodge his crafty assailant and facing imminent suffocation, Big Red John was forced to capitulate (in front of the whole forecastle) to London's demand to leave him alone for the remainder of the voyage. After routing Big Red John, his status went unquestioned for the rest of the voyage. No one trifled with the young wildcat from then on, and he even gained Big Red John's grudging respect in sticking up for himself.

One of the less fortunate crew members on board was a first-time sailor known as the Bricklayer, a forty-year-old landlubber from Missouri and the only crew member less experienced than London. The Bricklayer could not adjust to the sailing life and was incapable of mastering the most basic of sailing duties. He quarrelled with everyone and 'all hands had to do his work for him. Not only did he know nothing, but he proved himself unable to learn anything.'[6] His gross ineptitude and morose attitude made him despised by the other sailors and by the time they reached the sealing grounds, the Bricklayer had descended into a sulky isolation, loathed and shunned by all in the forecastle. He eventually took ill and, as London describes it, he 'died as he had lived, a beast, and he died hating us and hated by us'.[7] The Bricklayer was buried at sea with scant ceremony and no sorrow. His fate illustrated for London the deadly consequences for one who violated the integrity of the tribe. His petulance and incompetence desecrated the code of camaraderie and its mandates of cooperative grit and adaptability, behaviours that London had already identified as survival essentials. He had yet to read Darwin or Spencer, but it was no surprise that their ideas would resonate with him so intensely later on.

Life on the *Sophia Sutherland* was an intense struggle for survival. At the time, London was immersed in the immediate demands of this new unforgiving, raw environment, but writing later of the Bricklayer, he would offer a more complex and sympathetic view of the man's predicament: 'He could not, by the very nature of things, have been anything else than he was. He had not made himself, and for his making he was not responsible. Yet we treated him as a free agent and held him personally responsible for all that he was and that he should have not been. As a result,' London concludes, 'our treatment of him was as terrible as he was himself terrible.'[8]

Big Red John standing next to a Japanese woman, 1893, photographic print.

The complicated limits of agency and free choice would become persistent concerns in his writings. The impersonal interplay of intrinsic disposition and environmental circumstance seemed to dictate one's fate. How responsible were individuals for their shortcomings and failures? To what extent could one take credit for charitable deeds or worldly successes? London was starting to see that he was different than most – more intelligent, more vigorous, more determined – but also that somehow his robustness was, though innate, an arbitrary quality that compelled his determination to prosper where others failed. The voyage must have prompted him to contemplate his own destiny, as the *Sophia Sutherland* proceeded along a southern passage across the Pacific driven by the northeast trade winds towards Japan's Bonin Islands. En route, they sailed just north of the Hawaiian Islands. On deck London caught sight of Hawaii's volcanic landscapes and was awed by the precipitous mountain scenery. (Fourteen years later, as a renowned and prosperous author, he would sail his self-designed boat, the *Snark*, to Honolulu, where he would compose 'To Build a Fire', his most famous short story, about a prospector who freezes to death in the Yukon.)

After a 51-day passage across the Pacific, the *Sophia Sutherland* made landfall at St Johns in the exotic Bonin Islands. They would remain in the harbour for ten days refitting for their voyage north to the seal-hunting grounds. In transit, London had bonded with two Scandinavian sailors, Axel and Victor, and the trio, known as the 'three sports', made ambitious plans to explore the luxuriant, flower-filled jungles of the island's interior. London was spellbound by the magnificent gorges, cliffs, coral beaches and sparkling streams. 'I had won to the other side of the world . . . I was wild to get ashore,' he rejoiced.[9] But between the three sports and the verdant terrain lay a small coastal village. They had been at sea with no alcohol for nearly two months and decided to have a drink or two before hiking into the mountains. The trio quickly discovered that the village was overflowing with a diverse throng of riotous sailors from ships that were also refitting in the bay. They met up with some old acquaintances from San Francisco Bay and could not resist joining their fellow sea rovers for a few extra beverages. The mysterious alcohol they were served in square-face bottles was 'hot as fire, pale as water, and quick as death with its kick'.[10] Before they knew it, the normally even-tempered Victor had descended into a brawling alcohol-induced rage, and, with much difficulty, they corralled him back to the ship to sleep it off. Axel and London returned ashore and were enjoying the music of a Japanese orchestra in a tea house when Victor, who had somehow rallied with a vengeance, burst through a paper wall. Everyone, including the orchestra, fled through the nearest wall or door. Victor soon lapsed into a comatose stupor, but London and Axel soldiered on. Legions of sailors rollicked through the streets, more drinks were had, more stories were exchanged and more songs were sung. For London, 'the saturnalia was great. It was like the old days of the Spanish Main come back. It was license; it was adventure.'[11] He drifted along, lost track of Axel as he befriended other sea rovers and downed more drinks. The evening sank into a hazy blur, and London awoke the next morning in a doorway to find that his money, watch, coat, belt and shoes had been stolen. After their initial debauch, the three sports toned down their carousing, but they never made it past the village to climb the lava paths into the lush jungle before the *Sophia Sutherland* set sail for the sealing grounds to the Northwestern Pacific.

The harvesting of seals in the frigid waters off the coast of Siberia was a notoriously gory enterprise. The nineteenth-century northern Pacific fur seal industry initiated an unsustainable ecological catastrophe. In the 1860s Pacific seal herds numbered in the millions, but had already been substantially reduced by the year of London's trip in 1893. By 1910 the population of the Pacific fur seal would decrease to barely 140,000.[12] The harvesting of the seals was particularly brutal. They were hunted from small dories usually manned by a single hunter, a steerer and a puller who rowed the boat (London's job). The *Sophia Sutherland* had six such boats, from which the crew killed seals either in the water, by shooting them with shotguns as they migrated in concentrated groups, or on land, by clubbing them to death in their rookeries. Sealskin was used for trim on women's dresses and for muffs. It was also used to tailor fashionable men's motoring coats.[13] Typically, five sealskins were needed to make a motoring coat. In his novel *The Sea-Wolf*, London described seal hunting as 'wanton slaughter' and observed that no one

> ate of the seal meat or oil. After a good day's killing [the decks were] covered with hides and bodies, slippery with fat and blood, the scuppers running red; masts, ropes, and rails splattered with the sanguinary color; and the men, like butchers plying their trade, naked and red of arm and hand, hard at work with ripping and flensing-knives, removing the skins from the pretty sea creatures they had killed.[14]

The brutal hunting expedition lasted a hundred days, and when they sailed south towards Yokohama they ran straight into a violent typhoon. London himself was alone at the helm during the storm and – pitted against the raging elements – he safely steered the ship through the tempest for the duration of his watch. In Yokohama, they sold their haul of sealskins and spent two weeks in port. He spent most of his time in the waterfront saloons, but was able to see some of the city. They made a 37-day return passage across the Pacific and landed in San Francisco on 26 August 1893.

He returned to find the United States in a deep economic depression – the Panic of 1893. He also found that most of his old Oakland waterfront companions had disappeared, were dead or were behind bars. He used his pay-day money to buy some cheap

Jack London wearing sailor's attire in Yokohama, Japan, 1893, photographic print.

shirts and second-hand clothes. The rest went to his family to provide some much-needed financial support and to pay off their debts. For the time being, adventuring was over, and he moved back in with his parents. He also needed to get a job. With the economy in a disastrous recession, wages were low and jobs scarce. The only job he could find was in a jute mill, working for the same old 10 cents an hour. It was back to wage slavery and long hours, but he did find time for reading and the Oakland Public Library. He also spent some time at the YMCA, but though he found that environment healthful, the other boys he met there were too juvenile for his taste. More accommodating was the friendship he struck up with a young blacksmith apprentice named Louis Shattuck. Fancying himself a 'sophisticated townboy', Louis was practised in the rites and rituals of teenage courtship – a department in which London was sorely lacking.[15] The hyper-masculine world London had been initiated into on the waterfront and as a sailor was void of 'nice' girls. He readily admitted that adolescent courtship rituals were foreign to his being: 'I didn't know anything about girls. I had been too busy being a man.'[16] Together, Shattuck and London sauntered along the streets in the evenings meeting and talking to strolling pairs of girls. Determined to overcome his timidity and social awkwardness, London finally met a girl he called Haydee at a Salvation Army meeting. Though they only met a few times and stole perhaps a dozen kisses, he was smitten and for a short time came to 'know all the sweet madness of boy's love and girl's love'.[17]

Most of London's time during his first months back in Oakland was occupied by work, reading and his budding social life. When he visited the saloons it was only, he claimed, for their comfort and warmth – not drink. In October 1893 he also made his first foray into the literary arena. Encouraged by his mother and spurred by his own creative yen, he entered a young writer's contest in the *San Francisco Morning Call* and beat out university students from

Berkeley and Stanford to win the first prize of $25. His winning narrative, 'Story of a Typhoon Off the Coast of Japan', was a vivid recollection of the typhoon he had sailed through on the *Sophia Sutherland*. A contemporary critic described the prize-winning writer as both a reporter-adventurer and literary artist, praising his work's 'little touches of absolute realism that prove the author saw whereof he speaks . . . But the most striking thing is the largeness of grasp and steady force of expression that shows the young artist.'[18] The piece mingles elements of fact and fiction and is probably best classified as a work of autofiction – a hybrid genre in which the author's account is grounded in factual events but depicted through fictional methods and storytelling techniques. The creative contouring of actual experiences would become complex and varied in London's mature work, but as 'Story of a Typhoon' showcased, he displayed an inspired talent for creating a solid sense of 'I-was-there' authenticity. Early on, he had a sharp awareness of readers' fondness for fiction that seemed as 'real' as possible. He did submit more pieces to the *Morning Call* and, more ambitiously, to *Youth's Companion*, a national magazine, but they were all rejected.

He toiled on at his day job in the jute mill, but when the factory managers failed to come through with a previously promised payrise, he quit. He had decided that the juice of unskilled labour was not worth the squeeze, and single-mindedly set out to become an electrician. Electricity was certainly a growth industry, and London was still a believer in the work ethic and the ideal of upward mobility in the supposed meritocracy of American society. In accordance with the old American myths, he still trusted in the notion that a 'canal boy could become president' and 'any boy, who took employment with any firm, could, by thrift, energy and sobriety, learn the business and rise from position to position.'[19] Through his innate ability and determination he too would rise out of the socio-economic depths. 'I would carve my way to a place among [the upper classes] . . . I was not afraid of work. I loved hard work. I would pitch in and work harder than ever and eventually become a pillar of society.'[20] Enthusiastically, he applied to become an electrician apprentice at the local power plant. The interviewing superintendent noted the eighteen-year-old's naive eagerness and proposed that the best way for him to begin learning the electrical trade was from the bottom up. He would start London as a coal shoveller in the plant's powerhouse. For a monthly salary of $30, he would work ten hours a day, every day, with one day off per month. Exultant to finally be pursuing a trade, he accepted the offer. The proposed programme might be rough going at first, but it would pay off in the long run. Shovelling coal was gruelling and thoroughly sapped London's abundant physical vitality. He worked bone-grinding twelve- to thirteen-hour days, unknowingly doing the work of two men. He wrapped his sprained wrists in leather straps and soldiered on for a few weeks. Finally, one of the plant workers took pity on him and revealed that the superintendent who hired him had fired two coal shovellers, who were each making $40 a month, and replaced them with London, at a mere $30 a month. For London, the ordeal became a telling embodiment of the exploitative ethos of capitalist enterprise: damn the workers! Do whatever it takes to reduce costs and raise profits. In the relentless pursuit of money at every turn, the ambitious businessman was, in London's mind, obliged to crack this crucial question: 'Since the great mass of men toil at producing wealth, how best can he [the capitalist] get between the great mass of men and the wealth they produce, and get a slice of it for himself?'[21] The system reduced the managers to conniving schemers and the workers to ill-used brutes. In this instance, he was the casualty of a cunning efficiency expert, and the con primed him to embark on a new odyssey eastward on the open road.

The nation's ongoing economic depression caused widespread bankruptcies and left millions out of work. In response, populist Ohio politician Jacob Coxey organized an army of unemployed men to march in protest on Washington, DC. Their aim was to petition Congress to allocate funds for road and infrastructure improvements and thereby provide work for many of the jobless. 'General' Charles T. Kelly led a West Coast contingent of 'Coxey's Army' of around seven hundred men out of Oakland. On 6 April 1894 local police rousted Kelly's men into railroad cars half a day earlier than their planned departure time, and London arrived too late to catch the train. But, bent on joining the adventurous working man's cause, he used his road-kid skills, riding the rails and hopping trains, eventually catching up with the rear regiment of Kelly's Army at Ames Monument in Albany County, Wyoming, on 17 April. He travelled with the marching army eastwards through Wyoming, Nebraska and into Iowa. The army, which had swelled to 2,000 marchers, was forced to walk long distances and endure frigid temperatures. London's shoes wore out and his feet became severely blistered. In Des Moines, with the railroads now refusing passage to Kelly's men, they resorted to building flat-bottom rafts and floating down the Des Moines River to the Mississippi. Drawing on his boating expertise, London helped to manoeuvre his group's raft, the *Pirate*, to the vanguard of the fleet, enabling him and his crewmates to skim off choice provisions and supplies laid out by townspeople in anticipation of the army's arrival. Their progress was sluggish, supplies were growing sparser and morale was sinking. On 18 May, London wrote in his 'tramp diary': 'We passed a miserable day on the water with a chilling wind & driving rain. In the afternoon we camped in Missouri where we passed a miserable night.'[22] In Hannibal, Missouri, on 24 May, a restless London groaned: 'We went supperless to bed. Am going to pull out in the morning. I can't stand starvation.'[23] The next day, he lit out on his own and four days later was in Chicago, where he picked up his mail at the post office, which included a letter from his mother in which she enclosed four greenbacks. He was able to buy clothes and shoes and stay overnight at the local Salvation Army for 15 cents – the first actual bed he had slept in for nearly two months. While in Chicago, he visited the site of the 1893 World's Fair. The ornate neoclassical buildings of the fair's 'White City' were officially closed, but London discovered them inhabited by homeless people – a sign of the times.[24] He took a steamer across Lake Michigan to St Joseph, Michigan, where he spent the next month with the family of Mary Everhard – his mother's sister. His aunt was quite taken with her footloose young nephew, who told her of his literary ambitions and entertained her with tales of life as a tramp. He took a train to New York and arrived in the afternoon of 28 June at Niagara Falls. He was enthralled by the magnificence of the waterfalls and admired them for several hours deep into the moonlit night before going to sleep in a nearby field. Early the next morning, he was trekking back towards the falls to see them again in the early morning light when a constable arrested him for vagrancy. He was escorted to the city prison and locked in an iron cage with sixteen other hobos. In a trial that lasted all of fifteen seconds, with no witnesses or jury, the judge sentenced him to thirty days behind bars. 'I started to protest,' recalled London, 'but at that moment his honor was calling the name of the next hobo on the list. His Honor paused long enough to say to me, "Shut up!" The bailiff forced me to sit down.'[25] London was outraged at being denied due process. Yes, he may have been a tramp, but he was an American tramp! When he claimed that his rights had been violated and that he needed to speak to a lawyer, he was laughed at. London later said that his 'patriotic American citizenship there received a shock from which it has never fully recovered'.[26] The prison record formally catalogued his sentence thus:

On June 29, 1894, one John Lundon [*sic*], age 18; Single: Father & Mother Living, occupation: Sailor; Religion – Atheist – was received at the Erie County Penitentiary, for a term of 30 Days, charge of Tramp, sentenced by Police Justice Charles Piper – Niagara Falls, New York; and was released on July 29, 1894.[27]

Though in the past he had run with some rough sailors and dodgy tramps, the prison population was like nothing he had ever experienced. The 'pen', he reported, was 'a common stews, filled with the ruck and the filth, the scum and dregs, of society – hereditary inefficients, degenerates, wrecks, lunatics, addled intelligences, epileptics, monsters, weaklings, in short, a very nightmare of humanity'.[28]

The physical confinement and psychological brutalities of the prison house sent emotional shockwaves through London's psyche. What else but incarceration could be so acutely antithetical to his questing temperament? It was a ghastly experience, and to survive – despite his budding social consciousness – he did what he had to do to make it through his thirty days. He partook in the corrupt system of graft, extortion and exploitation that prevailed on the inside. 'When one is on the hot lava of hell,' he argued, 'he cannot pick and choose his path, and so it was with me in the Erie County Pen.'[29] He was lucky enough to become a hall-man with the help of a seasoned convict he had met at the beginning of his sentence. The hall-men were prison trustees who were exempt from hard labour and enjoyed privileges not afforded to the general prison population. They primarily worked to assist the guards in regulating the other prisoners. The hall-men seldom needed to request help from the guards in supervising the movement of prisoners, 'except in a quiet sort of way', London explained, 'when we wanted a cell unlocked in order to get at a refractory prisoner inside. In such cases all the guard did was to unlock the door and walk away so as not to be a witness of what happened when half a dozen hall-men went inside and did a bit of man-handling.'[30] With deliberate vagueness, he adds that the

man-handling was merely one of the very minor unprintable horrors of the Erie County Pen. I say 'unprintable'; and in justice I must also say 'unthinkable'. They were unthinkable

How Jack London travelled on a passenger coach, as illustrated in the first edition of *The Road* (1907).

Eerie County Jail (left) and the Municipal Building, Buffalo, New York, early 1900s.

to me until I saw them, and I was no spring chicken in
the ways of the world and the awful abysses of human
degradation. It would take a deep plummet to reach bottom
in the Erie County Pen, and I do but skim lightly and
facetiously the surface of things as I there saw them.[31]

However horrid the depths may have been, London adapted as
necessary.

Truth was, he was doing what he needed to do to survive – while
devising a fairly ample margin for his own welfare in the process.
As he did when with Kelly's Army, London expediently sized up his
options in the pen and ultimately pursued what was in his personal
interest. In a pinch, social justice and solidarity among vagrants or
thieves took a back seat to individualism and self-preservation. In
his mind, perhaps that is how it had to be. If he was ever going to
prosper or make some kind of difference in the world, he first had
to stay alive. Beneath his apparent alliances with other prisoners
(or hobos), he was always out for himself, and that self-interest was
probably the key to his survival. Even given the topsy-turvy moral
climate of prison culture, one gets a strong sense that, despite
various explanations and rationalizations in *The Road*, London
remained ill at ease with his ethically ambiguous and exploitative
behaviours in prison.

Released from prison on 29 July 1894, London made his
way by rail to Washington, DC, toured the capital's sights and
monuments, and found work in a stable. In mid-August he headed
north to Baltimore. There he spent the next few days listening to
an assortment of street socialists and hobo philosophers espouse
social theory and debate politics in Druid Hill Park. He was
captivated by their erudition and depth of knowledge on a wide
range of topics. London then spent time in New York City, where
he was dismayed by the city's derelict slums, grim poverty and
extensive homeless population.

In addition to learning about radical politics and urban squalor at first hand, he also claimed to have cultivated certain fiction techniques beginning early on in his tramp adventures, and connected these to his later literary accomplishments. When begging for food or money on the road, as he explained, it was vital to size up potential benefactors accurately. As a hobo, his success – the next meal or an extra dime – depended on his storytelling ability. 'First of all, and on the instant,' he notes, 'the beggar must "size up" his victim. After that, he must tell a story that will appeal to the peculiar personality and temperament of that particular victim . . . The successful hobo must be an artist.'[32] Though this was far from the full story of his literary education, London claimed:

> I have often thought that to this training of my tramp days is due much of my success as a story-writer. In order to get the food whereby I lived, I was compelled to tell tales that rang true. At the back door, out of inexorable necessity, is developed the convincingness and sincerity laid down by all authorities on the art of the short-story.[33]

Furthermore, he remarks, 'I quite believe it was my tramp-apprenticeship that made a realist out of me. Realism constitutes the only goods one can exchange at the kitchen door for grub.'[34] This account could surely have some truth to it, but the anecdote itself – one that is habitually recited by London biographers – is a choice example of an artfully devised, after-the-fact mini-yarn he knew readers would readily absorb as straightforward autobiography. It certainly demonstrates that London did eventually become an ingenious literary raconteur.

From New York he journeyed in September to Boston, where he visited Bunker Hill, the Old State House and Paul Revere's home. By the middle of September he was up in Montreal, and from there headed west by train across southern Canada. He travelled through

Ottawa, Winnipeg and Calgary, ending up in Vancouver on the West Coast. From there he voyaged south to Oakland, aboard the steamship *Umatilla* – the same vessel that would ferry him to the Klondike Gold Rush in less than three years. He shovelled coal in the ship's stokehold to pay his passage and was back home in early December.

His outlook on life and society had altered significantly. 'As a tramp,' he stated, 'I was behind the scenes of society – ay, and down in the cellar. I could watch the machinery work. I saw the wheels of the social machine go around, and I learned that the dignity of manual labor wasn't what I had been told it was by the teachers, preachers, and politicians.'[35] He was finally coming to realize that the 'men without trades were helpless cattle. If one learned a trade, he was compelled to belong to a union in order to work at his trade . . . And when a workman got old, or had an accident, he was thrown into the scrap-heap like any worn-out machine.'[36] London resolved to bypass what he called the 'social pit' that trapped, drained and junked workers.[37] He would pursue a different career path. 'Brains paid, not brawn,' he concluded. 'I resolved never again to offer my muscles for sale in the brawn market. Brain, and brain only, would I sell.'[38] On his journey, he had been plunged down beneath the proletariat into 'what sociologists love to call the "submerged tenth"'.[39] London admitted that when he began his road odyssey he was a 'rampant individualist' who fulsomely believed in the virtue of hard work, but his worm's-eye view of society from the bottom of the social pit ignited his social conscience. Though still unaware of the socio-political label, he had been transformed into a 'Socialist'. 'I had been reborn, but not renamed, and I was running around to find out what manner of thing I was. I ran back to California and opened the books.'[40]

# 4

# Epic Stampede: From Student to Klondike Gold Rusher (1894–8)

It was in the Klondike that I found myself . . . There you get your perspective. I got mine.

Jack London[1]

When a man journeys into a far country, he must be prepared to forget many of the things he has learned, and to acquire such customs as are inherent with existence in the new land; he must abandon the old ideals and the old gods, and oftentimes he must reverse the very codes by which his conduct has hitherto been shaped.

Jack London[2]

By early December 1894 London was back in Oakland. He was a month away from turning nineteen, but he had already accumulated a diverse and colourful array of identities he would draw on throughout his writing career: child labourer, oyster pirate, waterfront tough, road kid, Pacific sailor, hobo-tramp, convict – and burgeoning political activist. 'Adventurous' remains the most popular adjective to describe London's life, largely because his teen years were so packed with escapades and odysseys. And the prime adventure of his early life – the Klondike Gold Rush – was still more than two and a half years in the future. That exploit would help unify his creative energies and forever establish his authorial identity as the Northland's premier writer. The period between his 1894 road journey and his departure for the Klondike in 1897 would also be crucial. In that span he made his initial forays into more genteel social circles, explored new intellectual realms, briefly attended university, delved into reformist politics and made his first hard run at professional writing.

Fresh off the road in the waning days of 1894, he had pressing matters that needed immediate attention – namely his teeth and his education. His dental health was an inflamed disaster zone. He had never owned a toothbrush and had already had several of his decayed teeth extracted while tramping with Kelly's Army. He was not only a habitual smoker but a chronic tobacco chewer, a habit that disgusted his stepsister Eliza. He informed her that he used the 'chaw' to dull his toothaches, and she ended up paying for his much-needed dental work. And, on the condition that he quit the 'chaw', she bought a partial upper denture for his missing front teeth. Dental issues would plague him throughout his life, and periodontal disease exacerbated the kidney problems that would come to cause his death.

For the time being, John London's health had improved somewhat, and he was now working as a special official for the Oakland police.[3] His job, combined with income Flora was earning from her sewing and piano instruction, allowed London to go back to school and work only part time. John and Flora had moved into a cottage on Twenty-Second Avenue and Flora helped to arrange a comfy study-den for her son, replete with a bed, chair and desk, reading lamp and dresser. When he started attending Oakland High School in January, the burly nineteen-year-old cut something of a shaggy, proto-grunge figure. As a fellow student recalled, his 'face was ruddy and sunburned, and his tawny, disheveled hair looked as though he constantly ran his fingers through it. His general appearance was unbelievably shabby, careless and uncleanly, unlike anything I had ever seen in a school room.'[4]

He did various odd jobs during the spring term, including janitorial work at the school, but he also participated regularly in the Henry Clay Debating Society and in 1895 published nine articles and one story in the student literary journal *The Aegis*. Through the debating society, London became fast friends with Ted Applegarth. Ted's father was a mining engineer and the well-to-do Applegarth family provided London with an entrée into upper-middle-class refinement. Ted's older sister – the ethereally elegant Mabel – became one of his first major sweethearts and was partly the inspiration for the titular protagonist's love interest, Ruth Morse, in his semi-autobiographical 1909 novel *Martin Eden*. With gracious pedantry, she schooled him in the nuances of grammar and encouraged the voluble and excitable ex-sailor to modulate his tone and tame his frenetic gesturing. London would even accompany the Applegarths on their family holiday to Yosemite Park in the summer of 1895.

While he was being exposed to the niceties of Victorian decorum in the Applegarth home and reading poets such as Tennyson, Browning, Ruskin and Arnold with Mabel, he was also vigorously patronizing the Oakland Public Library. Later that summer he met the librarian and Christian-Socialist Frederick Irons Bamford, who helped mentor him as he read works by Herbert Spencer, Karl Marx, Charles Darwin and others. He was also influenced by raucous street philosophers in City Hall Park, where he heard the hobo-philosopher and socialist Frank Strawn-Hamilton harangue rowdy crowds. London did not officially join the Socialist Labor Party of Oakland until April 1896, but he had not forgotten his working-class tribulations. His article 'What Socialism Is' was printed in the *San Francisco Examiner* on 25 December 1895. In this, he put forward an inclusive definition of socialism as an all-embracing term. Communists, nationalists, collectivists, idealists, Utopians, and Altrurians are all socialists; but it cannot be said that socialism is any one of these, for it is all. Any man is a socialist who strives for a better form of Government than the one he is living under. Socialism means a reconstruction of society with a more just application of labor and distribution of the returns thereof. It cries out, 'Every one according to his deeds!' Its logical foundation is economic; its moral foundation, 'All men are born free and equal,' and its ultimate aim is pure democracy.[5]

For the most part, London's political outlook in the coming years corresponded to the general contours of socialist principles, but, at times, his commitments and viewpoints could stray from official Party policy. His definition here, however, is not as eccentric as some have claimed. Phil Gasper points out, 'Marx and Engels sometimes use this term [socialism] in a very broad sense to mean any concern for the social problems generated by capitalism.'[6] Much of the quibbling over London's socialist orthodoxy by scholars and historians has more to do with the perpetual demonization of the term by the conservative right in America than with London's actual activism or political opinions. As his celebrity grew in the coming years, socialists counted on him as a powerful ally. This alliance prospered not because his pronouncements meticulously followed the particulars of the movement's day-to-day agenda or because he proposed specific legislative remedies to social ills, but because the popular media willingly disseminated the famous author's anti-capitalist, pro-socialist and pro-labour sentiments to a mass audience receptive to the opinions of the writer-adventurer Jack London. And he, of course, had a knack for articulating socialist propaganda in clear and cogent language that a general audience could readily understand.

A half-length seated studio portrait of Jack London holding a cigarette in his left hand, 1896, photographic print.

He made it through the autumn semester at Oakland High and returned for the 1896 spring semester. But he was growing weary with the sluggish pace of the curriculum. To bypass wasting two more years in high school, he dropped out and enrolled in W. W. Anderson's University Academy in Alameda. Known as a 'cramming joint', the academy offered an accelerated study programme that prepared students to pass the entrance examinations to the University of California at Berkeley. Eliza chipped in for the pricey tuition, and he was off to the academic races to pass the exams that were only four months away. The programme allowed him to advance at his own pace, but over the first few weeks he absorbed the material so rapidly that it alarmed the academy's staff and annoyed his fellow students. The sloppily dressed working-class boy's academic prowess was putting the school's more affluent clientele to shame. The administration feared that word of his dramatic development might adversely affect the school's accreditation. The headmaster caved to the awkward optics of London's exceptional progress and discharged him from the academy with a full tuition refund. The expulsion infuriated London. Was he not striving to better himself like all good Americans should? Some part of him still clung – and always would – to the idea that hard work coupled with natural ability was the formula for success, but this was yet another real-world lesson in how the beneficiaries of class privilege did not take kindly to scruffy upstarts who refused to stay in their places. He had run headlong into the pernicious mix of class prejudice and academic elitism. He was caught simultaneously in the class warfare Marx wrote about and the struggle for survival espoused by the Darwinians. It is not difficult to see how the metaphor of struggle – clearly the keynote of London's early years – would come to permeate his work. 'The dominant theme', claims Joan London, 'of all his writings was struggle – the struggle of an individual to survive in a hostile environment or to be successful against great odds, and the bloody struggle of the workers against the capitalist class.'[7]

Society seemed a pitiless antagonist bent on pressing him down into the anonymity of squalid wage-slavery. To hell with them! He was not out to merely survive. He wanted to surge. London had not yet read Nietzsche, but he already exuded that philosopher's ethic of aspirational self-mastery. He decided to study for the exams on his own and enlisted the instructional assistance of two friends who were also studying for the exams. Fred Jacobs tutored him in physics and chemistry, while a young woman named Bess Maddern helped out with mathematics and grammar. (In 1900 he would, rather impetuously, marry Bess.) Dedicating himself to a stringent nineteen-hour-a-day study regime, he embarked on a quest to pass the entrance tests. 'For three months I kept this pace,' he explained,

> only breaking it on several occasions. My body grew weary, my mind grew weary, but I stayed with it. My eyes grew weary and began to twitch, but they did not break down. Perhaps, toward the last, I got a bit dotty. I know that at the time I was confident, I had discovered the formula for squaring the circle; but I resolutely deferred the working of it out until after the examinations. Then I would show them.[8]

The hard work paid off. He passed. Immediately afterwards he went sailing for a week to relieve what he called a 'splendid case of brain-fag'.[9] He set out from Oakland in a small boat to indulge in some restorative Bay cruising, stopping along the way to carouse with a few old drinking buddies from his oyster-pirating days.

A few weeks later he enrolled as a special student at Berkeley. That first semester he took courses in physics, algebra, geometry, English and u.s. history. An old Cole Grammar School classmate, James Hopper, met up with him one day on campus. Then an upperclassman and varsity football player, Hopper was impressed by the freshmen's youthful vivacity:

[London] had a curly mop of hair which seemed spun of its gold; his strong neck, within a loose, low, soft shirt was bronzed with it; and his eyes were like a sunlit sea. His clothes were flappy and careless; the forecastle had left a suspicion of a roll in his broad shoulders; and he was a strange combination of Scandinavian sailor and Greek god, made altogether boyish and loveable by the lack of two front teeth, lost cheerfully somewhere in a fight . . . He was full of gigantic plans – just as, indeed, I was to find him always whenever I came upon him later in life . . . He was going to take all the courses in English, all of them, nothing less. Also, of course, he meant to take most of the courses in the natural sciences, many in history, and bite a respectable chunk out of the philosophies.[10]

Despite an energetic start, London's collegiate career ended abruptly with an honourable dismissal in early February 1897 when he could not come up with the funds to pay his tuition. Instead of moping around, he threw in with the local Socialist Party to mount a protest against an Oakland city ordinance that banned public speech in Oakland without written consent from the mayor. To test the ordinance's constitutionality, London gave a speech in City Hall Park to deliberately incite his own arrest. Already known as the 'boy socialist', he garnered additional notoriety in the Bay Area for his principled defiance.[11] After acting as his own lawyer at his trial on 18 February, he was acquitted.

His socialist profile had been bolstered locally over the past year in the *Oakland Times*, which had published several of his letters on socialism, monetary issues and tax policies. These publications, along with his award-winning 1893 'Story of a Typhoon' and his string of *Aegis* articles, helped to give London the resolve that spring to embark on a full-time writing career. Borrowing an old typewriter, he hammered out an abundant variety of works that he submitted haphazardly to magazines and newspapers. 'Heavens, how I wrote!' he recounted. 'At times I forgot to eat, or refused to tear myself away from my passionate outpouring in order to eat.'[12] This early literary sally lasted about three months. The editors rejected his submissions, and once again London needed to find work to help support his family.[13] In the spring he was back to manual labour, working in a steam laundry at Belmont Academy, a boarding school south of San Francisco. The job was exhausting and left London scant time or energy for reading and studying, let alone writing.

Making matters worse, he was informed during this period that John London was not his biological father. Most likely, he learned about the controversy surrounding William Chaney's abandonment of his mother during her pregnancy from John London's relatives. He did some research in the San Francisco newspaper archives, which corroborated the story of his illegitimacy. This jolting revelation was profoundly upsetting. He wrote two letters to Chaney enquiring about his paternity, but Chaney wrote back in total denial, which only deepened London's consternation. Though he loved John London unreservedly and considered him his real father for the rest of his life, the shock of his 'bastard' status was a severe blow. 'He lived at a time when illegitimacy was regarded with horror except by the enlightened few,' remarked Joan London. 'It also seems probable that his knowledge determined his attitude toward his mother for the rest of his life. He was gentler to her thereafter, but he never quite forgave her. At the same time his affection for John deepened.'[14] Though his educational aspirations had been stymied, his writings rejected and his identity ruptured, London continued to submit his work for publication, but he was growing desperate.

Though the summer of 1897 started inauspiciously, it turned out to be a decisive turning point in his life. On 14 July the steamship *Excelsior* arrived in San Francisco, and a few ragged Arctic prospectors disembarked, packing walloping loads of gold. Word spread rapidly: gold had been discovered in the Far

North of Canada in the Klondike region of the Yukon. Straight off, thousands caught gold fever – dubbed 'Klondicitis' by the press – and were soon streaming north towards a new frontier in the Yukon in hopes of striking it rich.[15] London was one of these 'argonauts', and on 25 July he took off on a steamer bound for Port Townsend, Washington, where he boarded another boat to travel up the inside passage towards Juneau, Alaska.

He was accompanied by his brother-in-law James Shepard, Eliza's husband, who, much to London's good fortune, had caught gold fever himself. Eliza and Shepard mortgaged their house to finance the trip. At sixty years old, the ageing Shepard knew the 21-year-old London had the bodily stamina and adventurous spirit to help him bear the physical rigours of the journey. En route to Alaska, they prudently partnered up with three other men from Santa Rosa, California: Jim Goodman, an experienced prospector and hunter; Merritt Sloper, an able carpenter and seasoned traveller; and Fred Thompson, a California court reporter and the group's diarist.

In Juneau, the partners chartered two 23-metre (75 ft) Tlingit canoes to ferry them the last 160 kilometres (100 mi.) to Dyea. The old coastal trading post of Dyea had become a main artery to the Klondike goldfields for thousands of fervid prospectors. Getting to the Klondike from the coast would be an epic two-stage trek. First, London and his companions would trudge up a formidable coastal mountain range on the Chilkoot trail and crest the Chilkoot Pass, located 26.5 kilometre (16.5 mi.) to the east. From there, they hiked to Lake Lindeman. The journey's second stage consisted of manoeuvring a hastily constructed boat down a 885-kilometre (550 mi.) series of lakes, torrents and rivers that would carry them deep into the Yukon. This segment was less strenuous than the Chilkoot Trail, but presented its share of precarious rapids and navigational hazards. There was no time to dawdle. London and his party were frantically working to outpace the looming Klondike winter and the 'freeze-up' that would soon render the waterways impassable by boat.

Packers ascending to the summit of Chilkoot Pass during the Klondike Gold Rush, 1898, Eric A. Hegg, photograph.

Hiking the Chilkoot Trail, London had to carry his gear in stages, incrementally lugging individual loads ranging from 27 to 70 kilograms (60 to 150 lb) per trip. It was a gruelling haul. What made the trek so punishing was the recurrent backtracking needed to advance his hefty gear, load by load, between trailside encampments over rubble-strewn terrain that was mud-slicked, ever-steepening and littered with the putrefying corpses of dead pack horses. When the horses had floundered on the rough terrain or become enfeebled from lack of forage, they had been abandoned or shot by their owners. The heavy autumn rains, high winds, fog, snow and even oppressive daytime heat worsened the gold prospectors' miseries. At times, London stripped down to his red flannel underwear to avoid overheating. It did not take the newcomers – 'cheechakos' in Northland parlance – long to understand why old-timers described the Chilkoot as 'the worst trail this side of hell'.[16]

London's self-assurance and determination flourished in this rugged environment. As he recounted, 'I was twenty-one years old, and in splendid physical condition. I remember, at the end of the twenty-eight-mile portage across Chilkoot from Dyea Beach to Lake Lindeman, I was packing up with the Indians and out-packing many an Indian. The last pack into Lindeman was three miles. I back-tripped it four times a day, and on each forward trip carried one hundred and fifty pounds. This means', he specified, 'that over the worst trails I daily travelled twenty-four miles, twelve of which were under a burden of one hundred and fifty pounds.'[17]

Initially, the party traversed about 8 kilometres (5 mi.) up the Dyea River – towing their gear upstream on multiple trips in a small boat London had bought onsite for $10. By 12 August 1897, they were 13 kilometres (8 mi.) inland, slogging through the mud and rain along the winding canyon path as they pressed towards Sheep Camp. A flare-up of rheumatism rendered Shepard incapable of continuing, and he headed back to California. In his stead, a man named Martin Tarwater joined the group and proved adept at mending shoes and cooking. They were 6.5 kilometres (4 mi.) from the Chilkoot Pass at Sheep Camp on 21 August and over the next four days made their way to Stone House, 3 kilometres (2 mi.) up the trail. They arrived at the last camp at the foot of the Chilkoot Pass, known as the Scales, on the 27th. The Scales was 300 metres (1,000 ft) above the tree line at an elevation of 840 metres (2,750 ft). This basin of flat ground was the staging area where prospectors mounted their final, precipitous ascent to the Chilkoot Pass. The climactic stretch to the Chilkoot Pass appeared to ascend almost straight up. It rose a staggering 300 metres in just over a kilometre. Winning the summit, they plodded and back-tripped the remaining overland route down to Lake Lindeman, where they set up camp. Mindful of the encroaching Northland winter, they hurriedly started cutting timber for the construction of a riverboat to navigate a series of lakes and rivers that would take them to the Klondike and to Dawson City.

London's group pitched in with another party to build their boats. In twelve days they built two functional but leaky sister vessels, the *Yukon Belle* and the *Belle of the Yukon*. On 21 September both sailed from Lake Lindeman, with London piloting the squared-sailed, 8-metre (27 ft) *Yukon Belle*. At the tiller, he took advantage of swift winds, making good time on Lake Bennett, as they ferried through rough water that had capsized other boats, drowning several prospectors in the icy waters. They proceeded efficiently down the Tagish and Marsh lakes, entering the upper Yukon, known as the Lewis River, on 24 September. Thompson wrote in his diary: 'Sailed from Marsh Lake to the Lewis River, arriving at the river about noon, cooked our dinner on the boat, and drifted and rowed down the river, having a very pleasant afternoon, – found good camp for night on the river bank. Jim [Goodman] shot 2 pheasants.'[18]

The crew of the *Yukon Belle* faced a perilous hazard when they approached Box Canyon, which was halfway down the 95-kilometre (60 mi.) waterway connecting Lake Marsh and Lake Laberge. Here the narrowing canyon boosted the water's velocity just as the coursing river made an abrupt turn – a topographical combination

A scow passing through the 'Miles Grand Canyon' on the Lewis River, Yukon Territory, 10 December 1897, F. D. Fujiwara, photograph.

that had already wrecked the boats and dreams of numerous Gold Rushers. They could risk everything and shoot the gushing rapids in a matter of minutes, or they could portage around. The portage was the safe and sure route, but it would cost them four days. Needing to beat the onrushing freeze-up and confident in London's boating skills, the party voted unanimously to run the rapids. London managed to avoid disaster and successfully piloted the *Yukon Belle* – laden with 2,250 kilograms (5,000 lb) of supplies – through the stretch of rapids in two minutes. Then, as London later wrote, he and Sloper 'walked back by way of the portage and ran a friend's boat through. This was quite ticklish, for the little craft was but twenty-two feet over all, and proportionately heavier than ours.'[19] A few kilometres downriver they approached the White Horse rapids. According to London, this section was more hazardous than Box Canyon:

Of the two the White Horse was more dangerous than the Box. Save for a few who had been drowned, it had never been run in previous years. It had been the custom to portage everything around, even to the boats, which were skidding along on spruce tree trunks. But we were in a hurry and rather enthusiastic over our previous good luck; so not a pound was taken from the boats.[20]

Again, his partners were gung-ho and placed their bets with London at the helm. As they ran through White Horse rapids, the *Yukon Belle* was, in London's words, 'headed directly for the jagged left bank, and though I was up against the steering sweep till it cracked, I could not turn her nose downstream'. He saw that the 'bank was alarmingly close, but the boat still had the bit in her teeth. It was all happening so quickly, that I for the first time realized I was trying to buck the whirlpool. Like a flash I was bearing against the opposite side of the sweep.'[21]

Before young Jack London steers the *Yukon Belle* through the deadly rapids and drifts on safely towards the Klondike goldfields, we should pause momentarily to consider the position of our spunky prospector. At this moment he is poised almost exactly at the halfway point of his life and is thrumming with youthful energy. All sorts of varied possibilities lay ahead. He could strike gold in a few weeks and be instantaneously rich. Or he could be stone dead in the next ten seconds – his skull pulverized against a half-submerged boulder. Neither happened, of course, but the image of Jack London expertly threading the Yukon rapids offers an exquisite *in medias res* snapshot of the fledgling author. Both gutsy and reckless, such derring-do epitomizes his questing temperament that was forever pursuing an exalted rush. In his fiction, he would become particularly adept at capturing the ecstatic intensity of life's peak moments. In the most quoted passage from his most famous novel, *The Call of the Wild*, London vividly describes a 'summit-of-life' moment when his canine protagonist, Buck, subsumed by the 'tidal wave of being', pursues a snowshoe rabbit across the tundra:

> There is an ecstasy that marks the summit of life, and beyond which life cannot rise. And such is the paradox of living, this ecstasy comes when one is most alive, and it comes as a complete forgetfulness that one is alive. This ecstasy, this forgetfulness of living, comes to the artist, caught up and out of himself in a sheet of flame; it comes to the soldier, war-mad on a stricken field and refusing quarter; and it came to Buck, leading the pack, sounding the old wolf-cry, straining after the food that was alive and that fled swiftly before him through the moonlight. He was sounding the deeps of his nature, and of the parts of his nature that were deeper than he, going back into the womb of Time. He was mastered by the sheer surging of life, the tidal wave of being, the perfect joy of each separate muscle, joint, and sinew in that it was everything that was not death, that it was aglow and

rampant, expressing itself in movement, flying exultantly under the stars and over the face of dead matter that did not move.[22]

For London, there was nothing like being fully immersed in an exalted mode of primal consciousness that banished the ordinary and revelled in gleeful rapture. The adrenaline high of shooting the rapids encapsulates the 'big moments of living' he craved.[23] Such longings were not sensible by conventional standards. If, like most, London had been more cautious, he may have lived a more serene life and made it beyond forty, but he was not one to conserve his energies. He was bent on guzzling down all life had to offer as quickly as possible. That is probably why once he took the *Yukon Belle* beyond the White Horse rapids, he walked back again and ran another friend's boat safely through. Why not? It made for twice the fun.

Strong winds delayed their ensuing 50-kilometre (31 mi.) voyage on Lake Laberge, but after some hard rowing they made it to the Thirty-Mile River on 2 October. They began to encounter significant accumulations of slush ice – the river was starting to freeze up – but they ploughed on in a dense fog. With temperatures growing more frigid, they began averaging around 80 kilometres (50 mi.) a day, cruising past Little Salmon River, the Five Finger Rapids and Fort Selkirk. On 9 October they arrived at the Stewart River and settled into an empty cabin on nearby Split-Up Island. They were about 130 kilometres (80 mi.) from Dawson City. London and Jim Goodman did some prospecting over the next few days and on the left fork of Henderson Creek, London staked claim 'No. 54'. Then he, Fred Thompson and two other companions headed to Dawson on 16 October.

In town, they set up their tent alongside the cabin of two brothers, Louis and Marshall Bond. London clicked with the Bonds, who were Yale graduates and mining engineers from Santa Clara, California. The Bonds had two dogs with them in Dawson. One of the dogs was a large St Bernard Collie mix, which was, coincidentally, named Jack. This 65-kilogram (140 lb) canine would become the model for Buck in *The Call of the Wild*. According to Marshall Bond, Jack was an exceptional dog who

> had characteristics of such fine excellence as to be called character. He had a courage that, though unaggressive, was unyielding; a kindness and good nature that the most urbane man in the world might have observed with profit, and a willingness to do his work, and an untiring energy in carrying it out. I have had too much loyalty and affection from dogs to doubt that they have souls if men have them.[24]

Bond goes on to describe London's distinctive way of interacting with his dogs:

> London liked these dogs, and particularly this one which I called Jack. His manner of dealing with dogs was different from anyone I knew, and I remarked it at the time with interest. Most people, including myself, pat caress, and talk in more or less affectionate terms to a dog. London did none of this. He always spoke and acted towards the dog as if he recognized its noble qualities, respected them, but took them as a matter of course. It always seemed to me that he gave more to the dog than we did, for he gave understanding. He had an appreciative and instant eye and he honored them in a dog as he would in a man.[25]

London spent a little more than six weeks in Dawson. Food was scarce and the town was overcrowded and polluted, but the place fostered a unique camaraderie among the Klondikers. Dawson was little more than a mucky, tumbledown frontier outpost, but it boasted a colourful assortment of saloons and dance halls that offered convivial retreats from the cold winter darkness. London made the most of these establishments, socializing and absorbing

Marshall Bond, Oliver H. R. La Farge, Lyman R. Cold and Stanley Pearce sit with two dogs in front of a log cabin in Dawson, Yukon, 1897. The dog on the left with Marshall Bond was the inspiration for the character Buck in *The Call of the Wild*.

the tales he heard from the old-timers. The element suited him. London's open nature and easy amiability endeared him to his fellow miners. As fellow argonaut W. B. Hargrave recalled:

> No other man has left so indelible an impression upon my memory as Jack London. He was but a boy then, in years . . . But he possessed the mental equipment of a mature man, and I have never thought of him as a boy except in the heart of him . . . the clean, joyous, tender, unembittered heart of youth. His personality would challenge attention anywhere. Not only in his beauty – for he was a handsome lad – but there was about him that indefinable something that distinguishes genius from mediocrity. Though a youth, he displayed none of the insolent egotism of youth; he was an idealist who went after the attainable; a dreamer who was a man among strong men; a man who faced life with superb assurance and who could face death serenely imperturbable. These were my first impressions; which months of companionship only confirmed.[26]

Another young gold rusher, Edward E. P. Morgan, remembered London's gregarious presence in the Dawson saloons:

> I first met London in a Dawson bar in the late fall of 1897 . . .
> London was surely prospecting, but it was at the bars that
> he sought his material . . . I remember him as a muscular
> youth of little more than average stature, with a weather-
> beaten countenance in which a healthy colour showed,
> and a shock of yellow hair, customarily unkempt and in
> keeping with his usual slovenly appearance. It seemed
> to me that whenever I saw him at the bar he was always
> in conversation with some veteran sourdough or noted
> character in the life of Dawson. And how he did talk.[27]

Dawson's eccentric troupe of trappers, hunters and maverick entrepreneurs had yarns a-plenty to spin – especially after a whisky or two. It was an optimal setting for London to accumulate a rich supply of literary material that would soon propel his fiction out of the creative doldrums.

On 3 December he returned to Split-Up Island and settled into the routines of cabin life. The frigid temperatures and frozen ground foiled any serious mining for London. With only two or three hours of daylight in winter, the close quarters of the cabin could get oppressive, and serious discord among the miners was not uncommon. London managed to get along pretty well with his cabin mates. He had grown accustomed to the often delicate protocols of fraternity during his time on the waterfront, as a sailor and as a road kid. Emil Jensen, the inspiration for London's character the Malemute Kid in *The Son of the Wolf*, commented: 'To [London] there was in all things something new, something alluring, something worthwhile, be it a game of whist, an argument, or the sun at noonday glowing cold and brilliant above the hills to the south. He was ever on tiptoe with expectancy.'[28]

Genial and engaging as he may have been, London's stay was not devoid of conflict. A squabble erupted when he damaged Merritt Sloper's axe while chopping ice at the waterhole outside their cabin. Sloper became incensed at what he perceived as his partner's carelessness. To remedy the situation, London took up residence in a nearby cabin with 'Doc' Harvey, E. H. Sullivan and W. B. Hargrave for the rest of his time on the island.

By spring he was exhibiting symptoms of scurvy due to the lack of fresh fruits and vegetables during the long winter. Subsisting on the usual miner's diet of bread, bacon and beans, he was not consuming enough vitamin C.[29] He suffered from a general lethargy and aching joints, and his gums were swollen and bleeding. Around late May or early June he and Hargrave disassembled their cabin and made a log-raft to float downriver to Dawson. In town, they sold the logs from the raft, along with some driftwood they had collected along the way, to a sawmill for $600. Jack received some treatment for his scurvy at Saint Mary's Hospital and was advised to leave the region to fully recover.

On 8 June, he began the journey home to California on a makeshift raft down the Yukon River with two other Klondikers, John Thorson and Charles Taylor. The trio would cover more than 2,400 kilometres (1,500 mi.), making their way to St Michael on the coast. They made the trip in three weeks, braving swarms of mosquitos, hunting geese and trading with Native Americans for salmon along the way. They passed numerous camps on the riverbanks, and on at least two occasions stopped to watch Native American dance and religious festivals. At one of the dances, London felt he was listening to a song that was 'evidently born when the world was very young, and still apulse with the spirit of primeval man'.[30] But he also witnessed less vibrant scenes. When they passed another Native American village, he noted: '10 P.M. Indian village, only old people left. The perpetual cry for medicine. Stoicism of the sufferers. Traces of white blood among the papooses everywhere apparent.'[31] Throughout his stay in the Northland, he encountered indigenous peoples whose cultures had been adversely affected and devastated by colonial incursion. Though he valued the skills and ingenuity of Native American peoples, his viewpoint was largely shaped by the imperial and racist attitudes that animated the 'adventurous' spirit which propelled European pioneers and prospectors ever westwards in search of wealth, land and resources. London's portrayals of indigenous peoples were more nuanced than most writers of his era, but his was the perspective of the colonial conqueror, and much of his work remains limited by imperial biases. His often-positive depictions of tribal cultures and his use of sombre 'vanishing primitive' tropes are distorted by what Renato Rosaldo calls 'imperialist nostalgia', through which 'agents of colonialism' display a problematic yearning 'for the very forms of life that they intentionally altered or destroyed'.[32]

When they reached Anvik in Alaska on 18 June, London's scurvy had worsened. In town, he was finally able to consume some fresh potatoes and tomatoes. At this point, he wrote: '[the scurvy] has now almost entirely crippled me from the waist down. Right leg drawing up, can no longer straighten it, even in walking must put full weight on toes. These few raw potatoes & tomatoes are worth more to me at the present stage of the game than an El-dorado claim.'[33] They arrived at St Michael on the Bering Sea on 28 June, where London caught a steamship heading south. He likely worked as a coal passer to pay his passage and eventually wended his way back to Oakland in late July 1898.

'I brought back nothing from the Klondike but my scurvy,' London later quipped.[34] He had returned with only $4.50 in gold dust in his pocket, but he now possessed a bulging cache of raw experience to mould into the stories that would lift him out of penurious obscurity and towards fame, wealth and literary acclaim.

5

# Writer at Work: Early Success, Love, Marriage (1898–1902)

Take your time; elaborate; omit; draw; develop. Paint – paint pictures and characters – but paint, paint, draw, draw. And take your time. Spend a day on a paragraph, or on ten paragraphs. Grab your motif, master it. Make it live, and sprout blood and spirit and beauty and fire and glamor.

Jack London[1]

Do I contradict myself?
Very well then . . . I contradict myself;
I am large . . . I contain multitudes.

Walt Whitman[2]

He returned to Oakland in late July 1898 to discover that John London had died back in October 1897. The stark new reality for the 22-year-old was that he was now the head of the London household. Financially, it helped that his mother was receiving some remuneration from John London's Civil War pension and was earning income from her work as a music teacher and seamstress. Adding to domestic expenses, though, Flora was now the caretaker of John London's six-year-old grandson, Johnny Miller, who was living with her.[3] London found himself in a familiar position: the pressure was on to pitch in, get a job and help support the family.

His scurvy now in check, he gave mining one last go in the Nevada goldfields in August, but returned empty-handed. In the autumn, he ended up working sporadically at various menial jobs around Oakland. He even took the civil service exam to qualify for a postal carrier position with the post office, but more intently than ever London was now focused on his writing.

Creatively and intellectually, he was rapidly evolving in complex ways. In part, his development as a writer over the next year was prodded by his ever-flagging finances. 'Some are born to fortune and some have fortune thrust upon them,' he proclaimed. 'But in my case I was clubbed into fortune, and bitter necessity wielded the club.'[4] He desperately needed the money, and he saw a writing career as a means to becoming a 'brain merchant' and escape the perpetual hardship and soul-numbing agony of manual labour.[5] The writing game was a viable business proposition to be pursued with a methodical professionalism. In this vein, he often asserted that writing was much like a regular day job in which industriousness and hard work were paramount. 'Dig is the arcana of literature,' he insisted. 'There is no such thing as inspiration and very little genius. Dig, blooming under opportunity, results in what appears to be opportunity . . . Dig is a wonderful thing, and will move more mountains than faith ever dreamed of.'[6] Throughout his career, he had no issue declaring that he wrote for the money. Art for art's sake be damned! He told his friend and fellow writer Cloudesley Johns: 'I am writing for money; if I can procure fame, that means more money. More money means more life to me.'[7] Or so it seems if we take London's many I-only-write-for-money statements at face value. In reality, writing and art were baked into his existence. The central activity of his life was his writing. Bigger pay cheques meant more opportunities for bigger adventures and wider-ranging experiential opportunities – which in turn fuelled his writing and broadened his creative resources. Furthermore, like many prolific authors, he was enigmatically compelled from within to write. He needed to do something with the stories in his head. He had to write. Jay Williams observes that the imaginative flow from London's inner being was torrential, and that he 'was troubled – that is, haunted – by his own creative power'. His imaginative visions often seemed to originate preternaturally from sources beyond, beneath or independent from his own self or will. It sometimes felt like a form of creative demonic possession. His meticulously scheduled writing regime provided some means of channelling the abundance of his creative energies and subduing his 'sense of hauntedness and dream states'.[8]

The stories may have been gushing out, but he still needed to sell his work; thus he avidly studied the contemporary commercial literary marketplace and gauged the tastes of popular audiences who read magazines and newspapers. Getting paid for a story, he reasoned, was the truest validation of its cultural and aesthetic worth. This may seem an odd sentiment coming from a socialist, but London was not about to be exploited by the prevailing economic system. 'The deepest values in life are today expressed in terms of cash,' he affirmed. 'That which is most significant of an age must be the speech of that age. That which is most significant today is the making of money.'[9] He would soon achieve some financial stability and eventually great fame and wealth, but pecuniary motives were only part of what drove his literary ambitions.

London's 'arty' disposition and his intellectual curiosity were deep-seated and enduring, but his bohemian side would soon become increasingly masked by the rugged 'outdoorsy' popular image he was in the process of branding. The reading public, especially in America, wanted adventurers, not scholars. At least since the publication of 'Story of a Typhoon' in 1893, he had to some degree conceived of himself as an author, and as he explored the commercial possibilities for his work in the latter months of 1898, a creative alchemy was transpiring within. The wide range of his constant reading – fiction, history, philosophy, political theory, evolution and sociology – was beginning to synergize with his raw experiences in the Northland, on the Oakland waterfront and as a cross-country tramp. The impetus to write was driven as well by memories of the acutely felt scarcities from his childhood, a time of want he was determined to leave behind. As commonly stated by biographers and critics, his expanding perspective was spurred on by the recent Northland trip, but it was also in many respects simply the continuing development of London's hyperactive imagination, questing temperament and writerly ambitions. As much as he needed revenue from his work, writing also provided an outlet for his psychological fervour. And though he deliberately set out to be a financially successful, popular writer, he also sought to plumb his creative depths and chart his own artistic path. He insisted that 'mankind is my passion, and the search after potentiality and the realization thereof, my hobby'.[10]

That autumn and winter he feverishly composed and posted a steady stream of poems, articles and stories to publishers. Editors rejected almost everything he submitted. He was becoming impatient and exasperated, but the force of his ambition is evident in a letter of 30 November that he wrote to Mabel Applegarth: 'I don't care if the whole present, all I possess, were swept away from me – I will build a new present; If I am left naked and hungry to-morrow – before I give in I will go on naked and hungry; if I were a woman I would prostitute myself to all men but that I would succeed – in short, I will.'[11] Within the next week, he got his initial break when the *Overland Monthly* accepted his story 'To the Man on Trail' for their January 1899 issue. The *Overland* was a prestigious Western magazine based in San Francisco with an illustrious past. Edited in its early days by the famous California writer Bret Harte, this celebrated serial had published Mark Twain, Ambrose Bierce and Ina Coolbrith. Due to the magazine's financial woes at the time, however, they could only offer London $5 for the story. The pay was underwhelming, but he accepted their terms. It was a solid start.

Jack London, *c.* 1900.

Relentlessly, London continued to study, write and submit his work, but by the time Christmas rolled around he had only garnered more rejections. By late December, he was undergoing a dark night of the writer's soul. He opined to Mabel that it was 'about the loneliest Christmas I ever faced – guess I'll write to you . . . No body to talk to. No friend to visit.'[12] A few days later, he confessed to her brother Ted that 'I have never been so hard up in my life.'[13] Sometime between 25 December and the end of the year, an obscure magazine called the *Black Cat* had accepted a science-fiction story he had composed back in 1897 entitled 'A Thousand Deaths'.[14] Not a major publication, but a positive result nonetheless. Then, on 16 January, the postmaster informed London that a $65-dollar-a-month postal carrier position was available – would he take it?[15] The job was a steady, respectable, middle-class occupation with retirement benefits. The proposition was tempting and put London at a crossroads. He wavered and asked the postmaster if he could defer the appointment until the next opening to see if his writing career was going to pan out or not. Nothing doing, replied the postmaster. Take it or leave it. He left it. London had not crested the Chilkoot Pass to end up carrying a postbag around town.

Ever self-confident, he sensed correctly that his writing career was on the upswing. His mother, too, encouraged him to see it through with his writing at this critical point. She knew the depth of her son's intellectual and storytelling capabilities, and was privy to his powers of concentration and resolve. Maybe it was the gamble that drew her, but betting on her son's success was well founded. The reading public, it turned out, was ready for a writer like her son. The national mood was moving away from Victorian sentimentality and into the strenuous age of Theodore Roosevelt and the Progressive Era.

In late February, he was elated to discover that the *Black Cat* would pay him the generous sum of $40 for 'A Thousand Deaths'. The acceptance boosted his morale and provided a smidgen of financial breathing room. He also arranged a deal with the *Overland* to publish a series of Northland stories. One of the *Overland* editors, James Howard Bridge, claimed that when he met with London, the young author 'looked like a tramp, and nothing like a man who could have written an acceptable story for Bret Harte's old magazine'.[16] The *Overland* would only pay $7.50 per story, but the magazine's editors agreed to prominently feature his stories and hype the youthful author's name. This high-profile exposure was precisely what he needed to showcase his writing at this point in his career. He continued scrutinizing the writer's market and reading widely. By this point he was familiar with works by writers such as Schopenhauer, Kant, Malthus, Huxley, Milton and Spinoza. In addition to the Bible, Homer, Shakespeare, Dante and the major Romantic and Victorian poets, he was also well versed in recent fiction by Conrad, Hardy, Kipling, Wells, Oscar Wilde and others.

In June, a major breakthrough came when the well-established East Coast magazine the *Atlantic Monthly* accepted his story 'An Odyssey of the North'. He would receive a plush $120 for this work. Even better, he had tapped into a propitious publishing alliance. The *Atlantic* was the premier magazine of the publisher Houghton Mifflin, and this Boston-based company would go on to publish London's first collection of short stories, *The Son of the Wolf*, in April 1900. By the end of 1899 he had published 24 poems, stories, articles and jokes.[17] The former grimy road kid was drawing praise from readers and critics alike and was beginning to make a legitimate living from his writing.

In his early *Overland* stories, London's style is both expressive and spare. He could readily deliver brawny realism, and he could also ascend towards more exalted lyrical extravagances. Stylistically, he cultivated an emotive realism, asserting that 'mine is not *realism* but is *idealized realism* . . . artistically I am an emotional materialist.'[18] A dynamic brew of energizing contradictions, his fiction expresses the delvings of an imaginative empiricist. More genteel critics complained that his work was excessively brutal and slangy, but the majority of reviewers and readers praised its dramatic boldness. His style – often described as forceful, robust and virile – conveyed the feeling that this was an author striving to express and illuminate everything with a cogent accuracy. The second Northland story published by the *Overland*, 'The White Silence', offers a notable example of London's style and thematic scope. As a trio of prospectors sled across the frozen tundra, he delivers one of his most memorable atmospheric tableaux:

> The afternoon wore on, and with the awe, born of the White Silence, the voiceless travelers bent to their work. Nature has many tricks wherewith she convinces man of his finity – the ceaseless flow of the tides, the fury of the storm, the shock of the earthquake, the long roll of heaven's artillery – but the most tremendous, the most stupefying of all, is the passive phase of the White Silence. All movement ceases, the sky clears, the heavens are as brass; the slightest whisper seems sacrilege, and man becomes timid, affrighted at the sound of his own voice. Sole speck of life journeying across the ghostly wastes of a dead world, he trembles at his audacity, realizes that his is a maggot's life, nothing more. Strange thoughts arise unsummoned, and the mystery of all things strives for utterance. And the fear of death, of God, of the universe, comes over him – the hope of the Resurrection and the Life, the yearning for immortality, the vain striving of the imprisoned essence – it is then, if ever, man walks alone with God.[19]

Such passages show that from the beginning he was writing more than mere adventure stories. These tales, though entertaining and sensational, are existential sagas in which the struggles of the Northland are apt analogues for the modern condition in which bleakness, isolation and hostility reign. Beauty, at best, is blank and austere; God, if existent, is impassive and distant. Redemption, such as it is in London's work, usually comes in the form of social solidarity. Cooperation, altruism, comradeship are ethical musts. From an evolutionary perspective, he posits these traits as prosocial and adaptive. Politically, they usually point towards socialistic values that emphasize community and interdependence.

From the start, his work is freighted with ideas gleaned from his extensive readings in evolutionary theory, sociology and philosophy. Darwin, Marx, Nietzsche and Spencer are formative influences, and the opposition of Social Darwinism to Marxism, along with conflicts involving Nietzscheism and Christian ethics, undergird the thematic cross-currents in his stories and novels. Still, he was keen to maintain a certain economy and directness to sustain narrative momentum. Advice given by a veteran journalist in London's short story 'Amateur Night' suggests his own style: 'Be terse in style, vigorous of phrase, apt, concretely apt, in similitude.'[20] And relevant as well is an editor's counsel in 'Local Color': 'Make it concrete, to the point, with snap and go and life, crisp and crackling and interesting.'[21] London maintained that his prose was a deliberate product of 'artistic selection' and a 'pictorial eye' that 'draw[s] a picture in a few strokes' rather than spoiling it by 'putting in the multitude of details'.[22] He was no literary minimalist, but he did recognize that a scene's 'true picture' is best 'thrown upon the canvas by eliminating a great mass of things that spoil the composition, that obfuscate the true beautiful lines of it'.[23]

Barely out of the gate as a professional writer himself, he was nonetheless eager to offer guidance to other aspiring writers. In his October 1899 essay in *The Editor*, 'On the Writer's Philosophy of Life', he discusses how the eclectic acquisition of knowledge shapes one's creative output and fosters '*originality*'.[24] London admits that his notion of a 'philosophy of life' for writers does 'not permit of a precise definition', nor is it a 'philosophy on any one thing'.[25] Rather than packaged doctrine, he advocates a broad but intense cultivation of a particular kind of evolving awareness. He encourages a mindset that can supplely engage (and fittingly depict) the rapidly changing, information-laden world of modern life. He advises that writers, intuitively and analytically, should be in a perpetual state of expansive fluidity, absorbing and evaluating everything that impinges on their intellects and senses. 'You must,' London instructs the serious writer, 'have your hand on the inner pulse of things. And the sum of all this will be your working philosophy, by which, in turn, you will measure, weigh, and balance and interpret to the world.'[26] 'What do you know,' he chides his colleagues, 'of history, biology, evolution, ethics, and the thousand and one branches of knowledge? "But," you object, "I fail to see how such things can aid me in the writing of a romance or a poem." Ah, but they will. They broaden your thought, lengthen out your vistas, drive back the bounds of the field in which you work.'[27] Ideally, the serious writer cultivates habits of perception and learning that are exploratory and cross-disciplinary, fusional and continuously subject to revision and amplification. London's approach argues for the indispensable value of critical thinking and the vital necessity of lifelong learning. (The virtues of a liberal arts education were never lost on this college dropout.) This proclivity for absorbing new information may also help to explain why his views, in various ways, were prone to shift over time. Many have found this intellectual fluidity problematic. Biographer Richard O'Connor, for instance, asserts that London was 'suffering from a confusion of the intellect'.[28] How could a socialist be such an individualist? How could a determinist depict heroic triumph? How could a materialist believe in the soul? Ideological consistency was not a prime objective for London. He was more interested in dramatizing the clash of conflicting ideas.

His reading kept him informed of the shifting political, scientific and economic energies that were reshaping the modern era, while his travels granted him an alternative set of perspectives on how those forces were actually affecting workers and those living on the socio-economic margins. He strove to integrate weighty ideas and issues in his work, but he also knew that, in the popular literary marketplace, he needed to captivate his readers with stirring plots and compelling characterizations. He bridged the serious–popular gap through a multi-layered fictional technique, which he concisely defined in a 1913 letter:

> There are tricks and devices I use – tools in the art. I build a motive – a thesis, and my story has a dual nature. On the surface is the simple story any child can read – full of action, movement, color. Under that is the real story, philosophical, complex, full of meaning. One reader gets the interesting story, the other sees my philosophy of life.[29]

His writing frequently offers multiple levels of narration and allusion. The diversity of London's interests, along with his willingness to write for mass audiences, gives his work an array of opposing thematic strands that remain perpetually relevant. Most prominently, these include humanity's precarious relationship to the natural world and its non-human inhabitants (see *The Call of the Wild* and *White Fang*), the ongoing challenges regarding economic inequality (see *The Iron Heel* and 'South of the Slot') and cultural clashes instigated by globalization (see the Pacific and Northland stories).

Conflict, fusion, duality and polyphony are mainstays in London's work and have made him a difficult writer for critics to pin down. His ideological plurality and thematic diversity aggravate scholars looking to tag him with a totalizing label or theory, but these are vital for a fiction writer whose work is driven by conflict. It was also crucial for a critical thinker and 'revisionary visionary' who was always seeking a more informed standpoint.[30]

Oppositional motifs and theoretical frictions also tend to characterize the course of his literary production from work

Cloudesley Johns,
*c*. 1900.

to work. London's propensity was to portray a particular
philosophical perspective in one work and then in a later work to
re-engage that standpoint from an opposing viewpoint. He would,
for example, advocate strenuously for socialism in essays such as
'Revolution' and 'The Scab', but then turn around and dramatize
the problems of socialist reform in *The Iron Heel*. Or he would
vividly portray Buck's primitivization in *The Call of the Wild*, and
then offer its thematic reversal in his depiction of White Fang's
domestication.

Also sensitive to the nuances of literary perspective, London
frequently gave literary counsel to his fellow writer and good friend

Cloudesley Johns during these early years. In one letter to Johns, London sounds like a creative writing workshop instructor when he emphasizes the fundamental distinction between 'showing' and 'telling' in fiction writing: 'Don't you tell the reader. Don't. Don't. Don't. But HAVE YOUR CHARACTERS TELL IT BY THEIR DEEDS, ACTIONS, TALK, ETC. Then, and not until then, are you writing fiction and not a sociological paper upon a certain sub-stratum of society . . . Don't narrate – paint! draw! build! – CREATE!'[31] Always intent on creating a distinct ambience in his stories, he continues in this letter to elaborate on the necessity of agilely evoking a distinctive 'atmosphere':

> And get the atmosphere. Get the breadth and thickness to your stories . . . The reader, since it is fiction, doesn't want your dissertations on the subject, your observations, your knowledge as your knowledge, your thoughts about it, your idea – but put all those things which are yours into the stories, into the tales, eliminating yourself . . . and this will be the atmosphere, and this atmosphere will be you, don't you understand, you! you! you![32]

He understood that indirectness and implication were the engines of fiction. Action, characters and setting, rather than didactic narration, best advanced the story's plot. Early on, he also established a work routine that he would follow for the rest of his life. He wrote in the mornings, usually starting at around six or so and finishing up at about noon. He maintained his schedule diligently but not absolutely. He often claimed to faithfully write 1,000 words a day, but in practice his writing routine was not so rigid. Sometimes he wrote 1,000 words, sometimes more and sometime less, and he did not consistently write everyday. As London scholar Dan Wichlan's research has shown, from 1898 until his death on 22 November 1916, London actually produced an average of five hundred words per day, generating a total of approximately 3.5 million words spanning 53 separate volumes. (Notably, during the last eighteen months of his life London's output did increase to 1,000 words a day.)[33]

In late December 1899 he signed his contract for the publication of *The Son of the Wolf*, and for the first time in his life he was on his way to establishing some legitimate financial stability. In 1899 he had earned $388.75 from his writing. In 1900 his income would jump to $2,534.13.[34] As his literary reputation began to grow, his circle of friends and intellectual associates was also expanding. Around the Bay Area, he frequently gave lectures and attended events and gatherings where he rubbed shoulders with local literati, bohemians and academics. At a Socialist Labor Party meeting in December 1899, he met a striking Russian emigrant of Jewish descent named Anna Strunsky. She was a nineteen-year-old student at Stanford. He was captivated and so was she. Strunsky later acknowledged that it was love at first sight when she met London that evening. 'He seemed', she wrote, 'the incarnation of the Platonic ideal of man, the body of an athlete and the mind of a thinker.'[35] Anna herself dressed stylishly, was exceeding intelligent, politically progressive and positively alluring. One acquaintance described her as having 'soft brown eyes, a kindly smile and a throaty little voice that did things to your spine'.[36] London became a frequent visitor in the Strunsky home and a close, intense friendship quickly developed. They corresponded regularly, spent hours reading to each other and ambled together in the California hills discussing politics and philosophy. When they met up one clear, warm day on the Berkeley campus at the end of March 1900, London was ready to propose marriage. But some indeterminate lapse in their communication occurred during this rendezvous. Apparently, a certain genteel diffidence on Anna's part combined with a hasty reaction by London foiled the prospect of matrimony. Years later in an unpublished memoir, written in the third person, Anna recounted this critical moment:

Anna Strunsky, *c.* 1900.

They felt the call of youth to youth, the hunger of the heart
for the beautiful and good which each was to the other.

There was a feeling of crisis between them – of
something nearer, sweeter about to be born.

This was love, he thought.

Then he heard her say that she would go away –
when her studies were done, to Europe, to Russia

to share the revolution beginning there.

    On Saturday, three days later, he was
married in Church to another.[37]

He seems to have construed Anna's talk of travelling abroad as a
dismissal of their possible marriage. A rash response ensued: four
days later, he suddenly and successfully proposed to Bess Maddern,
his former mathematics and grammar tutor from his Alameda
Academy days. Bess and he shared an enthusiasm for photography
and bicycling and had maintained a respectful friendship. Their
marriage was not founded on the whimsies of romantic love
or carnal attraction; rather, it was to be a sensible partnership
ballasted by reason, practicality and compatibility. As Clarice Stasz
explains: 'Both acknowledged publicly that they were not marrying
out of love, but from friendship and the belief that they would
produce sturdy children. Neither was sentimentalist, yet they were
confident that their mutual affection would grow over time.'[38]
London justified his decision to an editor friend, claiming: 'I shall
be steadied, and can be able to devote more time to my work . . . I
shall be a cleaner, wholesomer man because of a restraint being laid
upon me instead of being free to drift wheresoever I listed.'[39] They
married on 7 April, the same day *The Son of the Wolf* was released.

    The couple settled into a spacious home on East Fifteenth Street
in Oakland, and Bess was pregnant by the end of April.[40] At first,
Flora and Johnny Miller lived with the couple, but the arrangement
soon became prickly, and mother and nephew relocated to a
nearby cottage. In early June, London finalized an agreement to
write a novel for the publisher S. S. McClure, who agreed to pay
him a $125-a-month advance salary. The novel, *A Daughter of the
Snows*, would be published in 1902. Set in the Klondike, it featured
a strong female protagonist and a number of powerfully rendered
Northland scenes, but on the whole, it would turn out to be
overwrought and structurally flawed.

Jack and Bess London at the beach, 1902.

Bess and London's first daughter, Joan, was born on 15 January 1901. It was a difficult birth for Bess and London was initially disappointed that the baby was not a boy, but his chauvinism soon dissolved into happy contentment with his newborn child. 'I did so ardently long to be a father', he wrote to Johns two weeks after Joan's birth, 'that it seemed impossible that such a happiness should be mine.'[41]

Along with his rising success and celebrity, he was thriving socially and civically. In January 1901 he accepted the Social Democratic Party nomination for mayor of Oakland. He had little expectation of winning and ended up receiving only 246 votes, but the nomination allowed him to promote a third party that genuinely supported working-class interests and was unbeholden to corporate authority. He was also mingling regularly with a loose affiliation of artists and bohemians known as the Crowd. Among others, this group included the poet Joaquin Miller, the artist Xavier Martínez, the photographer Arnold Genthe and the music and drama critic Blanche Partington. London also eagerly

George Sterling, aka 'Greek', and Jack London on the dock, *c.* 1910.

embraced the era's 'physical culture' fitness craze and avidly partook in boxing, biking, swimming and fencing with friends. Another person connected with the Crowd, the well-regarded California poet George Sterling, would eventually become London's closest male friend. They met in the spring of 1901, and in contrast to the burly author, the svelte Sterling was something of an aesthete with a classical artistic bent, but their personalities gelled. London playfully dubbed Sterling the 'Greek', and the poet referred to London as 'Wolf'. They devotedly critiqued each other's work, and they shared compatible hedonistic tendencies as spirited revellers and immoderate drinkers. After lectures and card games, they sometimes indulged in hashish sandwiches and visited local brothels and saloons.

At the end of 1901, London made the editorial connection of a lifetime with George Platt Brett Sr, the president of Macmillan. English-born and an East Coast patrician, Brett was an innovative businessman and had also spent time ranching in California. Brett shrewdly recognized the youthful western writer's unique talent and creative energy. He wrote to London that he believed the author's writings 'represent[ed] very much the best work of the kind that has been done on this side of the water'.[42] Artistically, commercially and personally, Brett and London were soon simpatico, and beginning with the short-story collection *Children of the Frost*, Macmillan would remain London's primary publisher until the author's death.

In February 1902 the Londons moved to a larger, more secluded home in the Piedmont Hills overlooking Oakland and the San Francisco Bay. Though he was thriving professionally and socially, London's romantic affections for Bess were stagnating, and he was growing emotionally and sexually frustrated. Bess was more contented with their home life and relationship, but was not as engrossed with the Crowd as London was. A major issue was that he was still in love with Anna Strunsky – and she with him.

He had managed to remain friends with Anna after his marriage, and they had been collaborating on an epistolary novel that would be published as *The Kempton-Wace Letters* in 1903. The narrative unfolds through a series of letters between Dane Kempton, an older English poet, and a younger economics graduate student named Herbert Wace, who is engaged to a woman named Hester Stebbins. Strunsky wrote the letters by Kempton, an idealist who believes romantic love is the proper basis for marriage. Herbert Wace, whose letters were written by London, counters Kempton's idealistic views, claiming: 'Love is a disorder of the mind and body, and is produced by passion under the stimulus of the imagination.' Love, according to Wace, is merely the 'means for the perpetuation and development of the human type', and therefore marriage should be entered into dutifully under a logically arranged compact of 'sex comradeship'.[43] Cleary – and surely with a bit a self-parody – London was using his Wace persona, at least in part, to rationalize his marriage with Bess. In one letter, Wace (London) declares: 'Wherefore I marry Hester Stebbins. I am not impelled by the archaic sex madness of the beast, nor by the obsolescent romance madness of later-day man. I contract a tie which reason tells me is based upon health and sanity and compatibility. My intellect shall delight in that tie.'[44] In real life, London could not argue away his impassioned longings for Anna, nor could he reason his way into an amorously fulfilling relationship with Bess. Tellingly, the novel ends with Hester Stebbins breaking off her engagement with Wace so she can marry another man who truly loves her – romance prevails over rationality in the end. *The Kempton-Wace Letters* is indicative of London's penchant for dramatizing divergent viewpoints – especially when it came to the wide array of moral, political and psychological problems generated by the competing perspectives of scientific rationalism and metaphysical idealism. In the coming years, personally and in his writings, he would wrestle with the antagonisms of the head and the heart in a variety of ways.

As London and Anna's collaboration progressed during the spring of 1902, they grew closer and their desire for one another deepened. Ardently he expressed his profound unhappiness with Bess to Anna, and declared that he was prepared to divorce so that they could marry. Secretly, he proposed to Anna in early May, suggesting that they run off to New Zealand or Australia together. In the heat of the moment, she accepted.[45] The affair was approaching the boil when London left in July on an assignment for the American Press Association to report on the aftermath of the Boer War in South Africa. After he departed, Anna would learn that Bess was pregnant with London's second child – a fact that he had neglected to mention. Refusing, finally, to be a homewrecker, Anna informed London that their romance was over for good. By this time, late August, he was in England, where he was writing a new work of non-fiction. The Boer War project had been cancelled, so he had detoured to London to write an exposé on the impoverished conditions in the city's notorious East End slums.

The result was a tour de force of immersive journalism entitled *The People of the Abyss*. Published in 1903, the book – part sociological study, part reformist literature and part undercover reportage – delivers a visceral first-hand account of the hellish conditions endured by England's urban lower classes. Late in his life, London professed: 'Of all my books on the long shelf, I love most *The People of the Abyss*. No other book of mine took so much of my young heart and tears as that study of the economic degradation of the poor.'[46] He spent six weeks in the East End, investigating, researching and exploring the slums. Disguised as a stranded American sailor, he embedded himself among the down-and-outers, slum dwellers and vagrants. At times, he slept in homeless shelters and on the street. Of the destitute East Enders, he observes,

Jack London and 'Bert the Cobbler', taken while Jack was in London working on *The People of the Abyss*, 1902.

the 'slum is their jungle, and they live and prey in the jungle'.[47] 'I
am made sick by this human hell-hole called London Town. I find it
almost impossible to believe that some of the horrible things I have
seen are really so.'[48] He meets and recounts the tragic and doleful
fates of capitalism's victims: broken workers, deprived children,
ailing women and cast-off veterans. They are inhumanely used,
depleted and discarded by bungled political policies and economic
systems driven by the mandates of efficiency and fuelled by the
exploitation of the masses. In a chapter entitled 'A Vision of the
Night', he remarks that the downtrodden East Enders are the 'unfit
and unneeded! The miserable and despised and forgotten, dying
in the social shambles. . . . If this is the best that civilization can
do for the human, then give us howling and naked savagery. Far
better to be a people of the wilderness and desert, of the cave and
the squatting place, than to be a people of the machine and the
Abyss.'[49] The human-engineered catastrophe he witnesses in the
East End incites the most brutish qualities of humanity, making
depravity – not wildness – the order of the day. The distinction is
integral for London. Primordial regression can be vitalizing and
restorative – but the predatory practices of unbridled capitalism
evoke a degenerative rapaciousness. 'The urban environment,' as
Agnes Malinowska proposes, is represented in London's writing
as 'a new kind of undefeatable wilderness, now monstrous in its
hostility'.[50] Rather than releasing the wild, this urban netherworld
only perverts and twists it.

By London's own estimation, *The People of the Abyss*, which
featured many of his own photographs of East Enders, was an
objective documentation of social conditions and not a socialist
polemic. 'I merely state the disease, as I saw it,' he asserted. 'I have
not, within the pages of *that* book, stated the cure as I see it.'[51] In the
final chapter, he posits that the most humane and practical course
of action is to hasten the demise of an inefficient and inhumane
capitalist-industrial system that has 'drained the United Kingdom

of its life-blood' and 'has enfeebled the stay-at-home folk till they are unable longer to struggle in the van of the competing nations'.[52] 'In short, society must be reorganized,' he remarks, 'and a capable management put at the head. That the present management is incapable, there can be no discussion . . . Every worn-out, pasty-faced pauper, every blind man, every prison babe, every man, woman, and child whose belly is gnawing with hunger pangs, is hungry because the funds have been misappropriated by the management.'[53]

After completing *The People of the Abyss* in late September 1902, he set off on a trip through Europe, visiting Paris, Berlin and Venice. When he received word on 20 October that his second daughter, Bess ('Becky'), had been born, he started for home, arriving in California on 13 November. Some debts had mounted in his absence, and he struck a deal with George Brett for Macmillan to advance him $150 a month as he worked to complete six books for the publisher over the next two years. He needed the steady income to help maintain his immoderate spending habits, to support his family and to help out his ageing foster mother, Jennie Prentiss. In 1902 London earned a healthy $4,400.[54] Despite his ever-increasing earnings over the years, his expenses were continually on the increase. He simply was not one to put money aside or rein in his spending habits. His writing output would have to keep pace, but that would not be a problem for the habitually productive author.

In early December 1902, he started writing a story about a dog, finishing it in less than two months. He wrote to Brett: 'It is an animal story, utterly different from the rest of the animal stories which have been so successful.'[55] He deliberated over the title – *The Sleeping Wolf, The Wolf.* Finally, he settled on *The Call of the Wild*.[56] Jack London was about to become famous.

6

# *The Call of the Wild*: Celebrity, War, Divorce, Fame, Remarriage (1903–6)

Ask people who know me today, what I am. A rough savage fellow, they will say, who likes prizefights and brutalities, who has a clever turn of pen, a charlatan's smattering of art, and the inevitable deficiencies of the untrained, unrefined, self-made man who strives with a fair measure of success to hide beneath an attitude of roughness and unconventionality. Do I endeavor to unconvince them? It's so much easier to leave their convictions alone.
Jack London[1]

. . . it's all right for a man sometimes to marry philosophically, but remember, it's damned hard on the woman.
Jack London[2]

When he turned 27 years old on 12 January 1903, London had five published books to his name. His young-adult novel *The Cruise of the Dazzler* had appeared in 1902, as had his long Klondike novel *A Daughter of the Snows*. Three well-received collections of Northland stories had also been published, *The Son of the Wolf* (1900), *The God of His Fathers* (1901) and *Children of the Frost* (1902). Remarkably, these early collections featured some of his strongest, most enduring stories: 'The White Silence', 'In a Far Country', 'An Odyssey of the North', 'The Grit of Women', 'The

Law of Life', 'Nam-Bok the Unveracious' and 'The League of Old Men'. Professionally, he was much matured, having established important publishing contacts and an astute working knowledge of the literary marketplace. And though he would continue to evolve and experiment over the course of his career, he had already cultivated a distinct authorial identity and a viable literary aesthetic that imbued his work with a layered thematic complexity. He was now poised to take his career to the next level, and *The Call of the Wild*, completed in late January 1903, would thrust him into the upper reaches of literary fame and critical approbation. His marriage with Bess, however, was descending into turmoil. They would endure an unpleasant separation in 1904, following his smouldering romantic affair with the less conventional and more freethinking Charmian Kittredge.

London sold the serial rights to *The Call of the Wild* for $750 to the *Saturday Evening Post*, which serialized the novel from 20 June to 18 July 1903. When George Brett of Macmillan offered to buy the rights to the book outright for $2,000, with a promise to promote the novel and its author though an extensive advertising campaign, London readily agreed. It seemed like a good deal at the time, but it guaranteed that he would never receive any future royalties on his best-selling, most durable work. Although the book's popularity turned the author into an international celebrity, Macmillan was the immediate financial beneficiary.

*The Call of the Wild* tells the story of the dog Buck, a 64-kilogram (140 lb) St Bernard Scotch Collie mix, who lives a stately life on Judge Miller's bucolic California ranch until he is stolen, sold to dog traders, and shipped north to the Klondike Gold Rush, where he is pressed into service as a sled dog. Life in the frigid Northland is brutal and unforgiving, but harsh conditions force Buck to tap into long-dormant instinctual drives that enable him to hold his own against the vicious dogs and hostile environment. He grows fiercely competitive and kills his chief rival, Spitz, becoming 'a dominant

primordial beast' and rising to the position of lead sled dog.[3] Buck
toils gamely for a series of sled-drivers until he is overworked by
abusive miners and is on the brink of death. He is rescued by John
Thornton, a self-reliant prospector who caringly nurses him back
to health. With Thornton and his partners, Buck journeys deep
into the wilderness, where he experiences further rewilding as his
primordial urges continue to intensify. After Thornton's death, a
thoroughly re-primitivized Buck joins and leads a feral wolf pack.

*The Call of the Wild* was an immediate hit with the critics and
the public. One reviewer summarized the novel as a 'clean, strong,
stirring story, well told'. A review in the *San Francisco Chronicle*
described it in dramatic terms: 'Fierce, brutal, splashed with blood,
and alive with the crack of whip and blow of club, it is yet a story
that sounds the deep note of tenderness between man and beast,
and that loyalty and fidelity that never falters.' The reviewer also
described London's work as 'strong meat for the anemic generation
that worships at the shrine of Henry James'.[4]

Over the decades, the novel has elicited a wide array of
interpretations. Donald Pizer reads it as an allegory of 'the
response of human nature to heredity and environment' that
blends parable and fable to suggest that 'man hovers between
the primitive and the civilized both in his make-up and in his
world, and it is his capacity for love which often determines which
direction he will take'.[5] Abraham Rothberg identifies a triple-tiered
structure to the novel. The narrative's first level delivers the story
of Buck, 'who reverts to type, learns to survive in wolf-like life, and
eventually becomes a wolf'. The second level is autobiographical
and suggests 'what London himself lived and felt climbing out of
poverty and deprivation to prestige as a writer and wealth'. And
the novel's third level is 'political and philosophical', one that
engages the implications of Darwinism.[6] Labor and Reesman see
the plot as 'animated by one of the most basic archetypal motifs:
the myth of the hero. The call to adventure, departure, initiation,

the arduous journey to the mysterious life-center, transformation and apotheosis . . . are present in Buck.'[7] Jacqueline Tavernier-Courbin acknowledges the novel's 'naturalistic, mythical, and archetypal characteristics' and offers a reading that emphasizes the narrative's romanticism.[8] She claims that the novel is 'romantic because of its emphasis on love, beauty, and justice, and because of its appeal to a complete range of emotions, from pity and anger to admiration and envy. It is also romantic because it dramatizes a human dream of adventure, freedom and personal fulfillment.'[9] Michael Lundblad discerns a 'homoerotic element' in Buck's relationship with John Thornton, which he reads as representative of 'queer desire between men', noting that London's work tends to 'both reinforce and resist broader cultural anxieties and alternatives in relation to alternatives to sexuality'.[10]

The novel's immersive pull originates with London's skilled use of a close third-person narrative perspective, which grants readers intimate access to Buck's inner life and infuses the story with a sense of psychological realism. Buck's canine musings and behaviours are much like our own, though more elemental. Uniquely, he is not simply a bundle of instincts wrapped in fur, but possesses an 'imagination' and sentient qualities that suggest some level of autonomy and self-awareness, though London stops short of merely anthropomorphizing his protagonist.[11] More radically, the narrative advances the Darwinian principle of an evolutionary continuity among species, and subverts conventional assumptions underlining the human–animal binary. As humans are (to some degree) instinct-driven animals, so too are non-human animals like Buck (to some degree) self-aware. The differences between canine and human are, after all, only ones of degree, not of kind. The novel is not disruptive in the usual political sense, but it does challenge traditional hierarchical relations between human and non-human animals.

It is also a tale of self-*re*discovery, which London conceives as a process of recollection stimulated by environmental change.

Buck adapts through an inner journey *back* into 'the womb of time' that manifests itself through a temperamental and physical revitalization.[12] As described midway through the novel's final chapter, Buck is well on his way to recovering his wildness:

> A carnivorous animal, living on a straight meat diet, he was in full flower, at the high tide of his life, over-spilling with vigor and virility. When Thornton passed a caressing hand along his back, a snapping and crackling followed the hand, each hair discharging its pent magnetism at the contact. Every part, brain and body, nerve tissue and fiber, was keyed to the most exquisite pitch; and between all the parts there was a perfect equilibrium or adjustment. To sights and sounds and events which required action, he responded with lightning-like rapidity . . . His muscles were surcharged with vitality, and snapped into play sharply, like steel springs. Life streamed through him in splendid flood, glad and rampant, until it seemed that it would burst him asunder in sheer ecstasy and put forth generously over the world.[13]

The 'snapping and crackling' and 'discharging' of 'pent magnetism' signify that Buck's primal instincts have been recharged through his contact with the primordial wilderness. London locates Buck's authentic selfhood beneath the civilized (dog) identity. One must, in short, lose the outer dog to find the inner wolf. As a primordial entity, the wolf is coherently synced with primal drives at the core of the self. For Buck, this process of rewilding is purgative, ennobling and viscerally enthralling:

> The blood-longing became stronger than ever before. He was a killer, a thing that preyed, living on the things that lived, unaided, alone, by virtue of his own strength and prowess, surviving triumphantly in a hostile environment where only the strong survived. Because of all this he became possessed

of a great pride in himself, which communicated itself like a contagion to his physical being. It advertised itself in all his movements, was apparent in the play of every muscle, spoke plainly as speech in the way he carried himself, and made his glorious furry coat if anything more glorious.[14]

Carnal regression, paradoxically, is not only liberating but ecstatically salvific. The novel maps a means (or fantasy) of recovering a former psycho-physical wholeness – a return to aboriginal holism. Such attractions to primitivism are almost always about recovering what one lacks or what one feels modern society has neutered or distorted. By the time Buck is leading the wolf pack at the close of the novel, it is difficult to conceive of his former domestic rompings on Judge Miller's ranch as anything other than prosaic and inauthentic. But Buck's existential journey out of the Southland to the Northland and into the wolf pack was not a path he freely chose. To recover his primordial self through a painful adaptive process, he had to be stolen and *forced* to undergo the agonizing and disorienting process of re-primitivization. Having grown soft on civilization's dubious values and decadent luxuries, dogs and humans alike are loath to leave their spurious comfort zones to answer The Call. The novel's warning to its mostly urban, post-frontier readership is to beware over-civilization. The comforts of 'cultural' progress are stifling, artificial and devitalizing.

As *The Call of the Wild* was about to be serialized that summer in the *Saturday Evening Post*, London was already actively at work on the novel that would become *The Sea-Wolf*. But he was becoming acutely restless in a marriage that was growing increasingly emotionally and erotically barren. To relieve some of the strain, Bess and their daughters went on holiday up in Glen Ellen at a rural summer resort named Wake Robin Lodge, about 80 kilometres (50 mi.) north of Oakland. They left Oakland on 11 June, and London planned to join up with them a week later, after spending some time on his new sloop the *Spray*, an 11.5-metre (38 ft) single-masted sailboat he had purchased in March for coastal and inland recreational cruising. A few days later, however, he was injured in a carriage accident, wrenching his knee and sustaining a number of cuts and bruises. Bess had asked a friend of hers and London's, Charmian Kittredge, to drop off some provisions at their Piedmont bungalow for London to bring to Glen Ellen. He and Charmian had first met back in 1900 through her aunt Ninetta Eames, who was connected with the *Overland Monthly*. Their interactions had been mostly fleeting and ill-timed, but their connection seems to have intensified during the spring and early summer of 1902. At a recent gathering of the Crowd, Charmian had bested London in a fencing match that was seriously competitive and palpably flirtatious.[15] When Charmian arrived at the bungalow on that day in June, she found London convalescing from his carriage accident. He was suddenly smitten, and as she was leaving he kissed her. The feeling was mutual and by 20 June their affair was, as London phrased it, coming along 'good and hard'.[16] From the start their relationship was deeply satisfying emotionally and physically. Early in July he was already writing gushingly to her: 'I am filled with a great pride. It seems to me somehow that all my values have been enormously enhanced. And do you know why? Because you love me. O God, that's the wonder of it, the wonder of it, that you should find me worthy of you!'[17] So much for the irrationality of romantic love! Any remaining notions of pragmatic coupling or rational matchmaking were flung aside. On 14 July he informed Bess that he was leaving her for someone else, but did not identify the other woman by name.[18] To sustain the secrecy of their affair, Charmian, rather deviously, maintained her friendship with Bess.

Charmian was much less conventional than London's previous major love interests. Just over four years older than London, she was athletic, musically talented, a connoisseur of the arts and frank with her sexuality. For two years she had attended Mills

Charmian London, *c.* 1905, photograph by Fred Hartsook.

Seminary and College and was a skilled typist, stenographer and efficient secretary. She exemplified the early feminist values of the 'New Woman'. Reformist and open-minded, this new generation of women was focused on leaving behind Victorian restraints and had dedicated themselves to carving out more active and independent female roles in public and professional spheres. Charmian's beauty was not traditional or delicate, but her charm, vivacity and intelligence made her attractive and appealing. She was proud of her shapely body, which was both strong and feminine. Neither prim nor modest, she dressed stylishly to accentuate her femininity, and played the piano beautifully. She was also an able hiker, swimmer, diver and equestrian. She boldly refused to ride her horse side-saddle, which was the female norm of the day; instead, she galloped blissfully through the California countryside fully astride her horse. Shocking! But she did not care. She exercised regularly and read avidly. Charmian's mother, Ninetta's sister and a minor lyrical poet, had died when Charmian was six, and Ninetta had become her guardian. A fervent freethinker, Ninetta had raised Charmian to be financially self-sufficient, conversant in the arts, socially broad-minded and sexually enlightened. Before marrying London, Charmian had enjoyed jointly fulfilling affairs with several Bay Area men. She was well read, outgoing, patient, loving, adventurous and self-possessed. (Their playful pet names for each other were 'Mate-Woman' and 'Mate-Man', or just 'Mate' for short.) The couple would have their rough moments, but the match proved remarkably stable and they remained together until London's death. Not an easy feat, given London's tendencies and behaviours, which were often self-centred, obsessive, addictive and sometimes dark, moody and depressive. Charmian would also occupy the central supporting role in his writing career, tirelessly acting as his erstwhile amanuensis – editing, typing, proofreading, mailing and archiving his manuscripts, letters and various documents.

Separated from Bess, he moved to Telegraph Avenue in Oakland, where he lived with his childhood friend Frank Atherton and his family. Through the autumn of 1903 he covertly continued his affair with Charmian. He worked regularly on *The Sea-Wolf* and completed several stories, including 'Love of Life', one of his best Northland tales, about an injured prospector's isolated struggle for survival in the Canadian Barrens. After accepting an offer from the Hearst Syndicate to cover the Russo-Japanese War, he boarded the steamship *Siberia* on 7 January 1904. He enjoyed the camaraderie with his fellow reporters on board, but it was also a frustrating passage. He came down with the flu soon after departure. Almost recovered when the ship stopped over in Honolulu, he managed to squeeze in a relaxing swim at Waikiki Beach, but back on board the *Siberia* he severely sprained his left ankle after an awkward misstep on deck. He couldn't walk for three days and had to hobble around on crutches for almost a week.

After arriving in Yokohama, he found that the Japanese authorities were not granting foreign correspondents permission to travel with the troops. To London, the restrictions were blatant censorship. He struck out on his own and travelled by train to Moji, but on 1 February he was arrested, fined and had his camera confiscated for taking photographs in the restricted fortified city. An American government official in Tokyo intervened and his camera was returned. (The photographs London took while covering the war – many of them portraits of refugees, children and the elderly – make up some of his most singular and affecting work as a photojournalist.) From Moji he caught a steamer and made his way to Fusan in southern Korea and took another boat that cruised to Mokpo on the southwestern tip of the Korean Peninsula. He needed to find a way to cover the next 290 kilometres (180 mi.) to Chemulpo (present-day Incheon) – a coastal city bordering Seoul on the east coast of Korea. This was where Japanese troops were disembarking to travel overland nearly 385 kilometres (240 mi.) north to the Yalu River, where they would do battle with the Russians on the border of Korea and Manchuria. To get to Chemulpo from Mokpo, London chartered a sampan, commonly referred to as a 'junk', which was crewed by three Koreans and also carried five Japanese passengers – none of whom spoke more than a few words of English. Sailing conditions were horrendous: frigid temperatures, high winds and stinging rains. The stormy weather damaged the junk's tiller and took down its mast. But they made it to Kunsan, where London was an odd curiosity to the hospitable locals who had never seen a Caucasian before. Cheekily, he wrote to Charmian, 'You should have seen me being made comfortable last night – five Japanese maidens helping me undress, take a bath, and get into bed . . . And this morning, same thing repeated – the Mayor of Kun San, the captain of the police, leading citizens, all in my bed-room while I was being shaved, dressed, washed, and fed.'[19] He chartered another junk on 11 February with a crew of five Japanese sailors. Through gale-force winds and heavy snowfall, they navigated the extreme 12- to 18-metre (40 to 60 ft) tidal changes while sailing between, around and over reefs and shoals. He described the junks as 'crazy' vessels made up of 'rags, tatters, rotten – something always carrying away – how they navigate is a miracle'.[20] When they made it to Chemulpo on 16 February, he began organizing an outfit with horses, cooks, grooms and interpreters for the journey to the Yalu River, where the Japanese and Russian armies were massing for battle.[21] By early March he was within 65 kilometres (40 mi.) of the front.

Jack London reprimanded by Japanese officers in Korea, 1904.

His 5 March dispatch, 'Cossacks Fight Then Retreat', reported on skirmishes between Russian scouts and Japanese forces. The article drew the attention of Japanese officials, who were perturbed that some maverick foreign correspondent had scooped a story of their military operations. They ordered him back to Seoul, where he spent the next month 'eating [his] heart out with inactivity'.[22] On 16 April London and a group of reporters were permitted to travel near the front, but their movements were highly supervised by Japanese officials. 'The chief duty of the officers looking after us,' he wrote, 'was to keep us from seeing anything.'[23] In one dispatch, bluntly titled 'Japanese Officers Consider Everything a Military Secret', he stated, 'I came to war expecting to get thrills. My only thrills have been those of indignation and irritation.'[24] He was disgusted with the officers for keeping reporters so far from the action and requested to be transferred to the Russian side in the hope of getting closer to the combat zone. But soon afterwards, he hauled off and punched a Japanese officer's groom for stealing feed reserved for his horse. He was arrested and detained for a court marshal. Potentially, the offence could have been punishable by death. The Japanese ended up releasing London, and by mid-June he was relieved to be onboard the *Korea* steaming towards San Francisco.

Journalistically, the five months he spent covering the war had been decidedly frustrating. He wrote to Charmian, '[I am] profoundly irritated by the futility of my position in this Army and sheer inability (caused by the position) to do decent work. Whatever I have done I am ashamed of.' Still, he managed to pen more than twenty articles and was the most intrepid and probably the most widely read Western correspondent to cover the war.[25] 'The only compensation', he felt, 'for these months of irritation is a better comprehension of Asiatic geography and Asiatic character.'[26] Though his experience of the Russo-Japanese War did not eradicate London's cultural or racial biases, it did upend and broaden his global perspective. He fully acknowledged Japan's superior military prowess and highly advanced organizational capacities. Its eventual victory over the Russians countermanded his notions of Western and Anglo-Saxon superiority. 'As a white man,' Daniel A. Métraux points out, 'he was a minority observing a war where Asia represented by Japan thoroughly outsmarted and overwhelmed numerically greater forces of the West represented by Russia. He soon realized that the West was not invincible, that Asians could through their own efforts defeat even Anglo-Saxons.'[27] Additionally, with Asia's ongoing industrial modernization, he recognized early on that China and Japan were rapidly developing economic and colonial powers that would soon rival and likely surpass Western dominance.[28]

Before he could get off the steamship in San Francisco, London was served separation papers from Bess on grounds of desertion and cruelty. (She also alleged that he had given her gonorrhoea.) In addition, she had placed a lien on his bank accounts and personal property, and the press had erroneously identified Anna Strunsky as the 'other woman'. Charmian, on the advice of her relatives, had retreated to Iowa with family to wait out the ensuing scandal, which was front-page news. On 11 November the court issued a divorce decree (with a mandatory one-year waiting period) on the grounds of desertion. Bess would retain custody of Joan and Becky and forego any rights to London's future royalties. He would provide a monthly allowance for her and the children and build them a new house on Thirty-First Street in Oakland. When the divorce was finalized on 18 November 1905, he and Charmian would be able to marry. Back in California during the summer of 1904, London was still struggling through a protracted depressive period dating from the previous year when his marriage was collapsing. He called it his 'long sickness', and would not 'recover' until well into 1905. This dark interval also amplified a more sceptical streak in his character, which he would express most fully in parts of *The Sea-Wolf, Martin Eden* and *John Barleycorn*.

The publication of *The Sea-Wolf* in October did introduce some positive professional news: the novel was a best-seller and critical hit. It continues to be the most widely read and the most frequently analysed of all of London's longer novels. Though some reviewers criticized its author's bloody realism, most found the narrative absorbing. Frederic Taber Cooper wrote in his review for *Bookman* that '[London] is by instinct a realist of such brutal strength that at times he is repellent. Yet even when you shrink from him, you are forced to concede his power.'[29] The *New York Times* called it a work of 'artistic and commercial' value, a 'stirring and unhackneyed tale of life on the high seas, full of the seafaring spirit'.[30] *The Sea-Wolf* opens on a foggy night when a ferryboat collides with a steamboat and passenger Humphrey Van Weyden, a literary critic and affluent man of leisure, is dumped overboard into San Francisco Bay. Fortuitously, he is rescued by Captain Wolf Larsen and brought aboard his schooner, the *Ghost*, which is headed across the Pacific on a seal-hunting voyage. Larsen refuses to return Humphrey

Jack London and his daughters, Joan and Becky, at an amusement park in California, *c*. 1905.

to San Francisco and presses him into service as a cook. He later becomes cabin boy and then is promoted to mate. Humphrey learns that Larsen is a self-taught, well-read intellectual. He is also a ruthlessly oppressive tyrant to the crew of the *Ghost*, which is a veritable hell-ship. Humphrey becomes Larsen's personal case study in human adaptability. The captain wants to find out if this scion of culture and privilege can survive the brutal conditions aboard the *Ghost*. Humphrey gradually adjusts to the crude shipboard environment. He toughens physically and becomes a proficient sailor, but he refuses to adopt Larsen's vicious tactics or concur with his nihilistic pessimism. His ethical stance gets a boost when the crew rescues shipwrecked poet Maud Brewster on the open sea. Together, she and Humphrey resist the demonic Larsen and escape the *Ghost* on an open boat, settling on the deserted Endeavor Island. Cooperatively, they cope with the elements and sustain themselves by hunting seals. Eventually, the hulk of the *Ghost* drifts ashore with only Larsen aboard. Abandoned by his crew, Larsen, who has been recurrently plagued by debilitating headaches throughout the novel, has grown blind as his condition has worsened. Still, he attempts to sabotage the efforts of Humphrey and Maud to repair the *Ghost*, but soon dies – blind, almost completely paralysed and defiant to the end. The novel closes as the surviving castaways are about to be rescued.

The novel's strength resides not so much with its plot, which relies on heavily improbable chance events, but in how London boldly shapes big ideas into what Keith Newlin calls 'a melodramatic battle between opposing philosophies' – namely individualism versus cooperation.[31] This opposition also reveals competing elements within London's own psyche in his depictions of Humphrey (the principled altruist) and Larsen (the selfish individualist). In part, London *is* Humphrey, the aesthete, the intellectual and the ethical idealist. He *is not* Humphrey, the naive 'sissy' with a private income. He *is* Larsen, the rational polemicist, tough-handed seaman and philosophical materialist. He *is not* Larsen, the violently oppressive sadist-psychopath. London's ethical endorsements hover somewhere between sissy and sadist. And though Larsen is one of the most absorbing characters he ever created, London is closer to Humphrey in psychological and emotional terms. The most difficult qualities to synthesize, however, are Larsen's philosophical materialism and Humphrey's ethical idealism. 'As I see it,' Larsen barks at one point, 'I do wrong always when I consider the interests of others.'[32] For Humphrey, Larsen's primary weakness resides in his flawed understanding of Darwinism. He rebukes Larsen: 'You have read Darwin . . . But you read him misunderstandingly when you conclude that the struggle for existence sanctions your wanton destruction of life.'[33] The ethical foundation of Larsen's materialism is actually a form of Social Darwinism. According to Larsen: 'Might is right, and that is all there is to it. Weakness is wrong.'[34] Carl Sandberg perceptively recognized Larsen as 'The System incarnate'.[35] The captain's sharply self-interested materialistic view is devoid of any redemptive moral imperatives or communal values. Life at its core is a sloppy, frantic melee governed by tumult and devouring. As he proclaims to Humphrey in Chapter Five:

> I believe that life is a mess . . . It is like yeast, a ferment, a thing that moves and may move for a minute, an hour, a year, or a hundred years, but that in the end will cease to move. The big eat the little that they may continue to move, the strong eat the weak that they may retain their strength. The lucky eat the most and move the longest, that is all.[36]

Larsen presents his arguments with enthralling charisma, but his individualism is more of an outgrowth of free-market capitalism than a mandate of humanity's biological ancestry. London posits a more selfless version of evolutionary theory through Humphrey and with the introduction of Maud Brewster, by depicting the behaviours of cooperation, reciprocation and altruism as more pro-adaptive and 'fit' than Larsen's reductive individualism. London seems at home with Larsen's materialistic epistemology but not with the might-makes-right worldview he derives from it. Maud and Humphrey's cooperative solidarity clearly triumphs over Larsen's egoism. The bottom line: Larsen dies, they live. But throughout much of the novel, Larsen out-argues and out-debates Humphrey, whose deficit is not so much intellectual as it is experiential. A product of class privilege, his problem is that he has never had to deal with the nuts and bolts of a real-world environment like the *Ghost*. He adapts to the crudities and brutalities of shipboard life, but he survives because he sustains enough cognitive autonomy to maintain a sound moral code that privileges mutual aid. Though surrounded by cruelty, he resists becoming cruel himself.

In addition to the lively exploration of evolutionary ethics through Humphrey's initiation into the world of the *Ghost*, *The Sea-Wolf* offers a revealing take on gender and masculinity. When Larsen learns that Humphrey lives off the fortune made by his father, he comments: 'You stand on dead men's legs . . . You couldn't walk alone between two sunrises and hustle the meat for your belly for three meals.'[37] Furthermore, Humphrey's muscles are 'small and soft, like a woman's' and when Larsen examines his hand, he proclaims it 'soft', pointedly stating 'dead men's hands have kept it soft. Good for little else than dish-washing and scullion work.'[38] For Larsen and the crew, Humphrey's want of 'hardness' denotes a lack of masculinity. Humphrey's ordeal aboard the *Ghost* will consist largely of establishing his position in the real-world dominance hierarchy of men. Larsen's attacks on Humphrey's masculinity align with the period's conceptions of manhood where, as Greg Forter notes, 'to be a man was to create oneself in the capitalist marketplace . . . The qualities that enabled such success were an aggressive assertiveness and competitive vigor thought of as innately male.'[39] Larsen sees Humphrey's servitude on the *Ghost* as an existential trial. 'It will be the making of you,' he tells Humphrey. 'You might learn in time to stand on your own legs, and perhaps to toddle along a bit.'[40] Masculinity must be earned, and because of his inherited wealth, Humphrey has never had to work for a living, making him a weak dependant rather than a rugged individualist who hoists his own sail. True, Larsen is the architect of Humphrey's initiatory rites, but just as he refuses to adopt the captain's ethics, Humphrey stops short of replicating Larsen's hypermasculinity. Larsen is a psychological cesspool of toxic masculinity. He is aggressively hostile, physically abusive, exceedingly competitive, paranoid and obsessed with control.

London had no qualms expressing his own masculinity, but he recognized the value of embodying traits that might be deemed, in a traditional sense, feminine. While he was writing *The Sea-Wolf* and in the early stages of his affair with Charmian, he wrote to her about his vision of the 'great Man-Comrade', a much longed-for, but never found, companion who was an 'all-around man, who could weep over a strain of music, a bit of verse, and who could grapple with the fiercest life and fight good-naturedly or like a fiend as the case might be'.

> This man should be so much one with me that we could never misunderstand. He should love the flesh, as he should love the spirit, honoring each and giving each its due. There should be in him both fact and fancy. He should be practical in-so-far as the mechanics of life were concerned; and fanciful, imaginative, sentimental, where the thrill of life was concerned. He should be delicate and tender, brave and game; sensitive as he pleased in the soul of him, and in the body of him unfearing and unwitting of pain. He should be warm with the glow of great adventure, unafraid of the harshness of life and its evils, and knowing all its harshness and evil.[41]

This was a man, he wrote, that 'I might merge with and become one for love and life'.[42] The letter conveys a complex array of desires. It offers an example of his dialectical habits of mind, and his penchant for synthesizing competing modes of being and ideas. The fusional ideal of the 'great Man-Comrade' also seems to be something of a narcissistic projection of London's conception of himself, which, among other things, allows this letter to function obliquely as a missive of self-revelation. (And perhaps also as a warning: Charmian, please be aware that I am really quite keen on myself – though this was something she doubtless already knew.) He could be expressing homosexual desire, and it also certainly reveals – given the letter's addressee – that he is strongly attracted to Charmian's 'New Woman' brand of feminized androgyny. Though Charmian and London were straight, cis-gendered individuals, they sometimes cultivated fluid, non-gender conforming or bi-gender attitudes and behaviours unusual for the times – especially when it came to athletic and outdoor pursuits (for Charmian) and artistic and empathetic undertakings (for London).

By December 1904 London was already at work on *White Fang*, a follow-up novel to *The Call of the Wild*, which would focus intently on themes of love and domestication. In February 1905 he set out on a six-week outing with Cloudesley Johns on the *Spray*. They were accompanied by Brown Wolf, London's new husky dog, and Manyoungi, a young Korean servant who had returned with the author from the Russo-Japanese War. (When critics scolded the socialist-writer for employing a valet, London shot back that Manyoungi's services gave him more time to improve his mind and fight for the cause.) In a symbolic gesture, he also accepted the Socialist nomination to run for Oakland mayor. (He received 981 votes.[43]) London was gaining more headlines and some infamy as a caustic socialist speaker around the Bay Area, and one of his finest collections of political essays appeared with the publication of *War of the Classes* in April 1905. That same month, he rented a cottage at

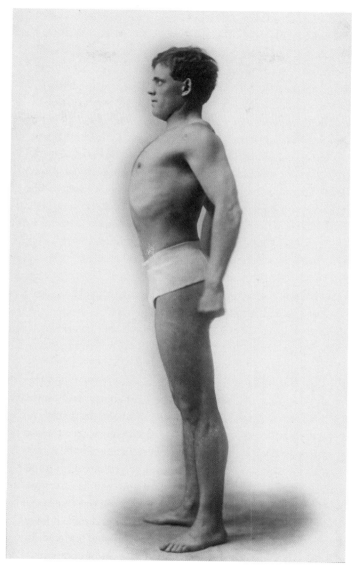

Jack London, semi-nude, *c.* 1904.

the Wake Robin Lodge resort at Glen Ellen, where he and Charmian were able to spend time together working on manuscripts, relaxing, swimming, horse riding, fencing and engaging in playful but hardy boxing matches with one another. On 4 June he made an initial payment on Hill Ranch. It was the first piece of land in Glen Ellen that would become part of Beauty Ranch, which he would eventually expand to more than 570 hectares (1,402 ac). In mid-October, he began a busy national lecture tour sponsored by the Slayton Lyceum Bureau. He spoke across the Midwest and on the East Coast. He talked about his travels and Klondike adventures but focused mainly on socialism, often giving speeches based on his essay 'Revolution'. On 17 November, while in Ohio, he learned that his divorce had been finalized. He met Charmian the next day in Chicago, where they were married. They continued the demanding lecture tour into December, and he spoke in Maine and at Harvard. The couple then went on a honeymoon to Jamaica, and also visited Cuba, Miami, the Everglades and Daytona Beach in Florida. He resumed the lecture tour, speaking in New York City before an audience of 10,000 people.[44] He also spoke at Yale and finished the tour in Grand Forks, North Dakota, returning to California on 9 February 1906.

Much of the fiery political rhetoric from his socialist speeches found its way into his socialist dystopian novel, *The Iron Heel*, which London started around the middle of August and finished on 13 December 1906.[45] This uniquely structured book was an important precursor for later dystopian novels, from George Orwell's *1984* to Margaret Atwood's *The Handmaid's Tale*. It is also his only novel that features a female narrator, Avis Everhard, who early in the book marries Ernest Everhard, the central socialist revolutionary figure of the story. Avis is the narrator of what becomes known as the 'Everhard Manuscript', a 'found document' that is discovered some seven hundred years in the future. This text is introduced, edited and footnoted by a scholar named Anthony Meredith in the year 419 BOM (Brotherhood of Man), a socialist utopian society. The 'Everhard Manuscript' supplies the central narrative whose main action takes place in the near future, covering the tumultuous years 1912–32. During this time, multiple socialist rebellions fail to depose the recently empowered Oligarchy, known as the 'Iron Heel'. Through violence and oppression the Oligarchy entrenches itself against the threat of socialist reforms and fends off their insurrections. Thematically, the novel proposes that socialism will never win the day through diplomacy. By whatever means necessary, elite capitalists will preserve their power and wealth against all attempts at legislative reorganization. The only way to wrest power from the Oligarchs is for the proletariat to rise up in violent rebellion against their economic overlords. In the book, this revolution takes some four hundred years to succeed. London's depiction of the vastly delayed triumph of socialism miffed his more sanguine political socialist allies. But history has not disproven the novel's glum assessments of power politics, greed and economic inequality. While London was writing *The Iron Heel*, one of his most popular works, *White Fang*, was published in October 1906.

London had written to editor George Brett back in December 1904 that he was planning a 'companion' novel to *The Call of the Wild*, in which he would 'reverse the process. Instead of the devolution or decivilization of a dog, I'm going to give the evolution, the civilization of a dog – development of domesticity, faithfulness, love, morality, & all the amenities & virtues.'[46] London explained the 'motive' of *White Fang* is that

every atom of organic life is plastic. The finest specimens now in existence were once all pulpy infants capable of being moulded this way or that. Let the pressure be one way and we have atavism – the reversion to the wild; the other the domestication, civilization. I have always been impressed with the awful

plasticity of life and I feel that I can never lay enough stress
upon the marvelous power and influence of environment.[47]

In relation to the novel, London also maintained: 'I am an
evolutionist, therefore a broad optimist, hence my love for the
human (in the slime though he be) comes from my knowing him as
he is and seeing the divine possibilities ahead of him.'[48] The novel,
however, depicts a more complexly conflicted portrait of civilized
existence than these comments suggest. Unlike *The Call of the
Wild*, this is not a story that culminates in escape and ecstasy, but
one that ends in compromise and repudiation. *White Fang* is less
pleasure principle and more discipline and punish.

Set in the frigid Northland wilderness, London's tale chronicles
the birth and development of a male wolf-dog hybrid, who is
eventually named White Fang. His father is a feral wolf and his
mother is half-wolf and half-dog. White Fang, then, is one-quarter
domestic dog and three-quarters wild wolf. The early chapters trace
White Fang's puppyhood adventures and portray his maturation
as a predator. These early chapters contain the novel's most cogent
descriptions of feral bliss, as when London describes White Fang in
pursuit of his prey:

> All the fighting blood of his breed was up in him and surging
> through him. This was living, though he did not know it. He
> was realizing his own meaning in the world; he was doing that
> for which he was made – killing meat and battling to kill it.
> He was justifying his existence, than which life can do no
> greater; for life achieves its summit when it does to the
> uttermost that which it was equipped to do.[49]

Soon, however, the 'dog' in White Fang is drawn to humans, when
he encounters the Native American Gray Beaver and his tribe.
He becomes domesticated and obedient, but endures a loveless

existence and is rejected by the other dogs in the Native American camp, who sense his wild-wolf heritage. White Fang is then acquired by Beauty Smith, a sadistic white man who trains him to compete in the dog-fighting arena, intensifying and perverting his natural ferocity. Eventually, a miner from California, named Weedon Scott, rescues White Fang from Beauty Smith and begins rehabilitating him through patience, love and kindness. The process is arduous. Scott's influence is working against White Fang's innate wolfishness and the cruelties endured during his time with Gray Beaver and Beauty Smith. Scott's gentle perseverance, care and nurturing do eventually elicit some affection from White Fang, but just beneath the surface resides the wolf – and an abused canine. After they move to California, White Fang gains the gratification of a supportive social network through Scott and his family, but lost are the powerful exaltations and instinctual raptures of his pre-human contact wild days in the Northland. White Fang's fate as a 'companion animal' is glaringly mundane. The novel ends as a litter of puppies he has fathered frolic about him. His predicament, though, is also very human. Domestication and civilization require an onerous degree of self-control and repression. '[White Fang] had to ignore the urges and promptings of instinct and reason, defy experience, give the lie to life itself.'[50] His new life may be secure and comfortable, but it is a profoundly inhibited existence.

While he was writing *White Fang*, London himself had been living the successful life of a financially flush celebrity and happily married man. But he was itching, as usual, for a new adventure. He was eyeing the western horizon on the Pacific Ocean. The South Seas were calling.

7

# To Build a Boat: The *Snark* Voyage, Hawaii, the South Seas (1907–9)

Fallible and frail, a bit of pulsating, jelly-like life – it is all I am.
About me are the great natural forces – colossal menaces, Titans of
destruction, unsentimental monsters that have less concern for me
than I have for the grain of sand I crush under my foot . . . It is good to
ride the tempest and feel godlike. I dare to assert that for a finite speck
of pulsating jelly to feel godlike is a far more glorious feeling than for a
god to feel godlike.

Jack London[1]

You have heard the beat of the off-shore wind,
And the thresh of the deep-sea rain;
You have heard the song – how long! how long!
Pull out on the trail again!

Rudyard Kipling[2]

On a summer's day in 1905, while lounging at a swimming pool
in Glen Ellen, London resolved once and for all to embark on a
round-the-world sailing voyage. Inspired in part by Joshua Slocum's
*Sailing Alone Around the World*, he began to plan out the trip and
design a sailing boat for the journey, one that would be named the
*Snark* (after the creature in Lewis Carroll's mock-epic poem 'The
Hunting of the Snark'). Following London's return from his lecture

tour, construction on the boat began in February 1906 at Anderson Ways shipyard close to Hunter's Point in San Francisco. 'Spare no money,' became his motto. 'Let everything on the *Snark* be of the best.'[3] It would be a 17-metre (55 ft) cutter-rigged ketch. He wanted it loaded with state-of-the-art amenities and constructed out of the best materials available. Among its many features, the vessel would have an ultramodern bathroom, ample headroom below decks and a custom 70-horsepower petrol engine. As usual, his ambitions were dramatically grandiose.

Never one to undersell his ideas, London's initial vision of the voyage was characteristically immoderate. 'This is something that has never been done before,' he exclaimed to one magazine editor. 'No writer of prominence, in the days of his prominence, has ever gone sailing around the world.'[4] Outlining the planned itinerary, he wrote: 'Hawaii is the first port of call [a 3,200-kilometre-plus (2,000 mi.) traverse from San Francisco]; and from there we shall wander through the South Seas, Samoa, Tasmania, New Zealand, Australia, New Guinea, and up through the Philippines to Japan. Then Korea and China, and on down to India, Red Sea, Mediterranean . . .'[5] Using its engine, the *Snark* could feasibly manoeuvre up major rivers such as the Nile, the Danube and the Seine. He would spend 'from one to several months' in every European country. 'There is no reason at all', he wrote, 'why I shouldn't in this fashion come up to Paris, and moor alongside the Latin Quarter, with a bow-line out to Notre Dame and a stern line fast to the Morgue.'[6] From Europe the *Snark* would cross the Atlantic to New York and then sail south around the Horn and back to San Francisco. In reality, the cruise ended up lasting only 27 months, ending after London was hospitalized in Sydney, Australia, for a double fistula and various tropical ailments.

Still, the challenge was exhilarating and provided him with a mass of subjects for his writing. In addition to *The Cruise of the Snark*, the trip inspired several of his finest stories, including 'The

House of Pride', 'The Chinago', 'Koolau the Leper', 'Good-by, Jack' and 'The Heathen'. During the voyage he also composed his most famous short story, 'To Build a Fire', and his most significant essay on animal behaviour, 'The Other Animals', as well as his semi-autobiographical novel *Martin Eden*, one of his most psychologically complex works. Even though the cruise was cut short, it delivered a plethora of 'big moments of living', as he put it, and was not a failure.[7] For most of the voyage, London's creative output, his marriage and his *joie de vivre* were integrated and flourishing as never before.

The planned voyage puzzled most of his friends. Why, they enquired, sail off into the Pacific wilds when your fame is peaking? 'Our friends', London protested,

> cannot understand why we make this voyage. They shudder, and moan, and raise their hands. No amount of explanation can make them comprehend that we are moving along the line of least resistance; that it is easier for us to go down to the sea in a small ship than to remain on dry land, just as it is easier for them to remain on dry land than to go down to the sea in the small ship.[8]

These naysayers, he continues, 'think I am crazy . . . It is a state of mind familiar to me. We are all prone to think there is something wrong with the mental processes of the man who disagrees with us.'[9] Though he maintained a regular work schedule, some degree of disequilibrium, novelty and the unknown was necessary to vitalize his existence. One way to gauge his peculiar disposition is merely to say, as many have, that Jack London craved adventure, and he did. But this continuous quest for extreme and varied stimulations seems inextricable from the ways in which he craved another cigarette, another trip to the library, the next drink or the completion of a new story. London's creative energy, his hunger

Jack London visits the *Snark* under construction, 1906.

for new ideas and experiences, and his famous derring-do were
largely compulsive. Instead of cautiously pulling back, he tended
instead to embrace his desires. 'The ultimate word is I LIKE,' he
proclaimed in the Foreword to *The Cruise of the Snark*. 'The things
I like constitute my set of values. The thing I like most of all is
personal achievement – not achievement for the world's applause,
but achievement for my own delight.'[10] London, who would be 31
when the voyage began, was still pursuing the new and the exotic
and was anxious to head once more into the great beyond. Even
though some of his political comrades were critical of the trip, he
saw it as a chance to extend rather than abandon the cause and
to bring his revolutionary ideas and speeches to international
audiences. Such an expedition, moreover, was a dream he had
cherished since childhood: a free, open adventure in his own boat!
Almost everything about the voyage was slapdash and impetuous,
but without London's impulsiveness, the *Snark* would have never
been built. Furthermore, he knew that risky enterprises fuelled

his literary output, and he was confident in his ability to work efficiently under spartan conditions. The dangers of the open Pacific were real and the cruise would be beleaguered by both petty irritations and serious hazards. But as long as he could write for a few hours each day, everything would be paid for. While he worked, most sailing and shipboard duties would be handled by the crew, although he would end up labouring at a number of nautical duties himself.

In addition to London and Charmian, the crew would consist of chief navigator Roscoe Eames, Charmian's sixty-year-old uncle and former Bay Area ferry captain. Nakata Tochigi, London's new Japanese servant who had replaced Manyoungi, served as cabin boy. The ship's cook was Kansan Martin Johnson, who would eventually become a famous documentary film pioneer. The position of engineer was filled by a Stanford student named Herbert Stoltz, a future Rhodes scholar and medical doctor. The cross-Pacific journey in a boat the size of the *Snark* required an exacting resilience. The make-up of the crew changed often on the trip, as members quit or were fired and replaced. Johnson was the only one to stay with London and Charmian for the entirety of the journey.

Getting out of port would be its own accomplishment. The building of the *Snark* and the first leg of the voyage were impeded by various delays and problems. The estimated cost was $7,000, but as one thing led to another, the boat ended up, according to London, costing $30,000. Many of the building delays and construction problems were caused by the San Francisco earthquake of 18 April 1906, the same day that the boat's 4.5-metric-ton iron keel was to be cast. After feeling the jolt that morning in Glen Ellen, London and Charmian ventured down to San Francisco that evening and watched helplessly as flames engulfed the city. The scene was apocalyptic. They could hear the sobbing and cries for help from people trapped in the rubble. Charmian wrote that seeing the vast destruction 'proved our closest to realizing a dream that came now and again to Jack in sleep, that he and I were in at the finish of all things – standing or moving hand in hand through chaos to its brink, looking upon the rest of mankind in the process of dissolution'.[11]

Despite ballooning labour costs in the aftermath of the earthquake, London pushed forward with construction of the *Snark*, but the interruptions and mishaps continued to mount. He had to deal with 'forty-seven different kinds of union men and with one hundred and fifteen different firms' over the course of the boat's construction.[12] Before it was even out of port, the *Snark* seemed to be breaking down faster than it could be repaired. It got pinned between two large barges and was almost crushed. Then, after the *Snark* had fallen between the ways in the shipyard, it took tugboats a week to dislodge it from the mud. Finally, even though the petrol engine was broken, the windlass inoperative and the interior unpainted, London decided it was better to depart with the vessel unfinished. They could make repairs and put the final touches to the boat more cheaply and efficiently in Honolulu. They departed on 23 April 1907 and quickly discovered that the *Snark*'s sides and bottom were alarmingly leaky. Even its ostensibly watertight compartments leaked, as did the lifeboat and the fuel tanks. They also found that the ironwork on the boat's rigging 'snapped like macaroni'.[13] The crew could not get the *Snark* to heave-to in order to stay steady in the rough seas. The result was more discomfort, labour and seasickness for everyone aboard. Their custom sea anchor also failed. 'On one occasion,' Martin Johnson admitted, 'I almost gave up, and expressed to Jack the wish that I could see land. He [London] replied: "Never mind, Martin, we are not over two miles from land now;" and when I asked him which way, he said: "Straight down, Martin, straight down."'[14]

And then things got worse. Roscoe, it turned out, did not know how to navigate. The main problem was that he was a disciple of Cyrus R. Teed's cosmological theory that the Earth was actually a concave sphere and the Sun was positioned at the centre of a globe that measured 12,800 kilometres (8,000 mi.) in diameter.[15] 'Roscoe believes,' London joshed, 'that the surface of the earth is concave and that we live on the inside of a hollow sphere. Thus, though we shall sail on the one boat, the *Snark*, Roscoe will journey around the world on the inside, while I shall journey around on the outside.'[16] Needless to say, they could not get an accurate reading of the *Snark*'s position. Fortunately, London was able to step in on the fly and teach himself celestial navigation from his onboard nautical guides. He was, miraculously, able to keep the boat on a correct route to Hawaii. On 17 May they sighted Maui and by 20 May they were in Pearl Harbor and into Pearl Lochs.[17] The 27-day crossing had nearly been a total disaster and had been filled with a slew of petty and not so petty irritations. They were fortunate to have survived.

In Honolulu, London started writing what would become his most acclaimed short story, 'To Build a Fire'.[18] It tells of the demise of a Klondike prospector who journeys alone with a husky dog across the snow and ice in temperatures that plunge below the 50-degree-below-zero mark. It may seem odd that London penned this coldest of stories in balmy Honolulu, but viewed in light of the recent near-fatal crossing he and the *Snark* crew had very luckily survived, the story reads like an exercise in literary atonement. With 'To Build a Fire' he discretely substitutes one deadly, indifferent and inhospitable setting (the Northland) for another (the Pacific Ocean). The story was partly inspired by his recent reading of Jeremiah Lynch's memoir *Three Years in the Klondike*, and London, of course, had not been sailing alone.[19] Still, given the story's prompt genesis on the heels of the *Snark*'s onerous crossing, it is difficult not to see 'To Build a Fire' functioning largely as a cautionary self-reminder that, from time to time, it might be wise for its author to rein in his daredevil tendencies. Moderation was not one of London's strong points, and his personal 'I LIKE' credo had its limits. His deeper urge may have been to break free into the great beyond and answer the

Jack London and crew navigating aboard the *Snark*, 1907.

call of the wild (like Buck), but he also needed (like White Fang) to find a way to temper his primal cravings.

The tone of 'To Build a Fire' is hauntingly dispassionate and understated. London's protagonist, a miner, is referred to impersonally as 'the man':

> He was a new-comer to the land, a chechaquo, and this was his first winter. The trouble with him was that he was without imagination. He was quick and alert in the things of life, but only in the things, and not in the significances. Fifty degrees below zero meant eighty-odd degrees of frost. Such fact impressed him as being cold and uncomfortable, and that was all. It did not lead him to meditate upon his frailty as a creature of temperature, and upon man's frailty in general, able only to live within certain narrow limits of temperature; and from there on it did not lead him to the conjectural field of immortality and man's place in the universe.[20]

Initially, it seems as though the man's concentrated focus might be a survival advantage: here is a mulish, technically minded individual absorbed in the task of making it back to camp to rejoin his partners. He proficiently notes distance, temperature, time and direction. The man, however, is efficient only in isolated particulars; he lacks 'imagination' or the capacity to anticipate or appreciate the contingencies of his predicament. The quantitative calculations that guide his decisions fail to remedy the predicament in which he has placed himself. The story suggests that the better mindset would be less instrumental and more meditative and conjectural – a 'big-picture' mode of thinking oriented towards fusing and unifying actions, needs, benefits and risks. Limited by his lack of imagination, the man is fixated on the immediate, the literal and the calculable. As a result, he fails to recognize his vulnerabilities as a solitary individual and dismisses the crucial pre-journey advice of the old-timer in the story who 'had been very serious in laying down the law that no man must travel alone in the Klondike after fifty below'.[21] In this tale of rugged individualism gone awry, disconnection is the man's prevailing malady. His arrogant self-centredness blinds him to his own limitations and isolates him from the old-timer, the environment, the husky and his partners.

Later in the story, when he breaks through the ice, soaking his feet, the man attempts to build a fire to thaw his rapidly freezing lower extremities. But his fire is snuffed out by melting snow that falls from an overhanging tree limb, and the numbing cold prevents him from restarting the fire, initiating a panicked spiral into a fatal hypothermia. As the cold begins to wrap and permeate the man's body, London eerily juxtaposes the indifferent macrocosm of the universe with the animate microcosm of the body: 'His pace of four miles an hour had kept his heart pumping blood to the surface of his body and to all extremities. But the instant he stopped, the action of the blood eased down. The cold of space smote the unprotected tip of the planet, and he, being on that unprotected tip, received the full force of the blow. The blood of his body recoiled before it . . . the skin of all his body chilled as it lost its blood.'[22] After the man dies, the husky catches 'the scent of death' and pauses to howl 'under stars that leaped and danced and shone brightly in the cold sky'.[23] Describing the stars with this touch of pathetic fallacy momentarily transgresses the story's naturalism, but it neatly reinforces a haunting sense that the universe gladly disposes of its incompetent spawn. The story's ecogothic vibe suggests that this world is somehow simultaneously indifferent *and* malevolent.

During their time in Hawaii, the Londons were able to settle down and enjoy some relaxing activities. London tried out surfing at Waikiki Beach and managed to catch a few choice waves. In the process, he acquired a grisly sunburn that rendered him bedbound for days. He wrote an article about learning to surf, entitled 'A Royal Sport', which ended up being a seminal promotional essay on the sport in the United States.

The Londons also spent a week visiting the leper colony on Molokai. They saw the disease as a dreadfully cruel fate but also quickly discovered that the frightful stories they had heard about the colony and its inhabitants had been grossly sensationalized and exaggerated. London found the lepers living on Molokai to be content. In 'The Lepers of Molokai', he candidly states that 'in Molokai the people are happy', and reveals that once lepers adjust to life on the island, they are loath to leave.[24] At the colony, what he witnesses is largely a socialistic commune in which poverty, class conflict and worker exploitation are non-existent. He contends that 'if it were given to me to choose between being compelled to live in Molokai for the rest of my life, or in the East End of London, the East side of New York, or the Stockyards of Chicago, I would select Molokai without debate'.[25] Additionally, he asserts: 'I have seen Hawaiians living in the slums of Honolulu, and, having seen them, I can readily understand why the lepers, brought back from the Settlement for reexamination, shouted one and all, "Back to Molokai!"'[26] London presents the settlement (though a product

The *Snark* with sails raised, docked in the Oakland Estuary, 1907.

of colonialism) as a rationally organized, humanely administered cooperative commonwealth in which equity, harmony and happiness flourish. While some fishermen, tradesmen and shopkeepers engage in free enterprise, the territory manages the settlement, and the social ills spawned by capitalism are conspicuously absent from this socialistic mini-state. In his assessment, even exiled lepers can enjoy fruitful and meaningful lives when emancipated from the woes spawned by the industrial free market.

The Londons stayed in the Hawaiian Islands for five months while the refitting of the *Snark* progressed. They toured various ranches and plantations and were entertained by prominent residents. Their trip up Maui's Haleakalā volcano inspired one of London's best descriptive travel essays, 'The House of the Sun'.

The *Snark* disembarked from Hilo on 7 October 1907, charting a southeast course for the Marquesas. It would be a desolate sixty-day passage, during which they never sighted another vessel. About halfway through, the crew discovered that a tap had been left on, depleting half the *Snark*'s water supply. London had to strictly ration the crew's daily water intake until a rain squall – the only one they encountered on that leg of the trip – replenished their supplies. Hydrated or not, the crew found the fishing spectacular. They caught dolphin fish (*mahi-mahi*), bonitas, sharks and a strange snake-like fish.[27] He noted that 'bonitas are the veriest cannibals. The instant one is hooked he is attacked by his fellows.'[28] Daily they watched the slaughter of multitudes of flying fish as they fled the ambushes from dolphins below only to be picked off by seabirds from above. 'It was sad to see such sordid and bloody slaughter,' he commented.[29] Nor were the humans aboard immune from Darwinian potencies on the open sea. He noted that 'in the night watches, when a forlorn little flying-fish struck the mainsail and fell gasping and splattering on the deck, we would rush for it just as eagerly, just as greedily, just as voraciously, as the dolphins and bonitas'.[30] They were immersed in appetite and struggle. London, once again, was in his element.

In addition to fishing, the crew found diversion in the five-hundred-book library London had stored away on the *Snark*. They played cards, sparred with boxing gloves on deck and listened to records on a phonograph. (He was particularly fond of opera.) The *Snark* finally arrived at Nuku Hiva in the Marquesas on the night of 6 December and stayed for twelve days. The island was literary holy ground for London. It was the setting of Herman Melville's 1846 novel *Typee*, a formative book from London's childhood that had enthralled him with its exotic depictions of cannibalism, high adventure and love in the lush South Seas paradise. At first, that paradise seemed intact when in the morning they 'awoke in a fairyland [and] the *Snark* rested in a placid harbor that nestled in a vast amphitheatre, the towering, vine-clad walls of which seemed to rise directly from the water'.[31] But upon closer inspection, they discovered that the now depleted indigenous population was no longer comprised of the strikingly robust people that had so captivated Melville. The surviving natives had been ravaged by diseases introduced by colonial Europeans. And they were almost all debilitated by asthma, elephantiasis, leprosy, tuberculosis or other maladies. 'Life has rotted away in this wonderful garden spot,' reported London, 'where climate is as delightful and healthful as any to be found in the world . . . When one considers the situation, one is almost driven to the conclusion that the white race flourishes on impurity and corruption.'[32]

Though he frequently criticized the disastrous consequences of imperialism on the *Snark* voyage, London also exhibited 'colonial ambivalence'.[33] He himself was a beneficiary of imperial expansion, and his Western values and prejudices inevitably distorted his impressions of Pacific cultures. Justin D. Edwards argues that London 'idealized Hawaii and condemned the colonial project that sought to corrupt the Polynesian Islands with "civilization"'. Edwards further explains that London is caught in a perceptual tangle as he 'critiques imperial projects and ostensibly renounces civilization while he simultaneously imposes Western values upon the foreign locale'.[34] Colonial oppression, nevertheless, is a prominent theme in London's Pacific fiction and is movingly portrayed in 'Koolau the Leper', a story he composed in May 1908.

Based on an actual occurrence, the story describes Koolau and his followers, an indigenous group of Hawaiians from Kauai infected with leprosy, who have been ordered by the Euro-American imperial authorities to be deported to the leper colony on Molokai to live out the rest of their days. The Kauaians, however, are determined to stay on their beloved home island and steadfastly refuse to leave. Rallying his followers in the beginning of the story, the defiant Koolau lays bare the hypocrisy and ulterior motives of the missionaries and traders who colonized the islands:

They came like lambs, speaking softly. Well might they speak softly, for we were many and strong, and all the islands were ours. As I say, they spoke softly. They were of two kinds. The one kind asked our permission, our gracious permission, to preach to us the word of God. The other kind asked our permission, our gracious permission, to trade with us. That was the beginning. Today all the islands are theirs, all the land, all the cattle – everything is theirs. They that preached the word of God and they that preached the word of Rum have fore-gathered and become great chiefs. They live like kings in houses of many rooms, with multitudes of servants to care for them. They who had nothing have everything, and if you, or I, or any Kanaka be hungry, they sneer and say, 'Well, why don't you work? There are the plantations.'[35]

The police land on the island and exchange deadly gunfire with Koolau and his rebellious followers, and all except Koolau end up surrendering after being shelled by a u.s. Navy boat. Koolau retreats into Kauai's lush and craggy interior, eluding his pursuers in the dense jungles for two years before he dies alone in a thicket: 'Free he had lived, and free he was dying.'[36] Thematically, the story is deeply anti-colonial, but it also shows that Koolau's heroic and righteous defiance has already been rendered futile.

Departing Nuka Hiva on 18 December, the *Snark* sailed on another 1,600 kilometres (1,000 mi.) to the southwest and arrived at Tahiti on 27 December. There they encountered the unique personage of Ernest Darling, 'The Nature Man'. London had actually met Darling once before on Market Street in San Francisco, remembering him as 'another prophet . . . come up to town with a message that will save the world'.[37] Darling had been a sickly youth from Oregon, but managed to rehabilitate himself through natural living – vegetarianism, nudism, nature and sunshine. 'To live, [Darling] must have a natural diet, the open air, and the blessed

Ernest Darling, 'The Nature Man', in Papeete (Tahiti), 1908.

sunshine' – and what better place to enjoy it all than Tahiti?[38]
Much to London's delight, he was also a socialist. Darling was a
refreshingly eccentric but principled character who believed he was
'in the world for the purpose of being happy and [had] not a moment
to waste in any other pursuit'.[39] Less entertaining was the pile of
post the Londons found waiting for them in Tahiti. Some financial
and banking matters had become muddled back in California.
Temporarily interrupting the cruise, London and Charmian booked

passage back to California on the steamship *Mariposa*. In California he socialized, addressed his finances, visited his daughters and departed back for Tahiti on 2 February 1908.

He finished his novel *Martin Eden* on 24 February in Tahiti and completed 'The Other Animals' on 19 March. He wrote that article in response to accusations of 'Nature Faking' by John Burroughs and U.S. President Theodore Roosevelt, which the pair had levelled at several contemporary writers of animal stories, including William J. Long, Ernest Thompson Seton and London. Roosevelt in particular had singled out the implausibility of certain scenes in *White Fang*.[40] Burroughs and Roosevelt had ganged up to deem the writers guilty of anthropomorphizing their animal characters, exaggerating the animals' mental capacities and misleadingly portraying animal behaviour. In his article, London shot back that Burroughs and Roosevelt were 'homocentric' in their view that non-human animals were merely instinctual 'automatons' capable of 'performing actions only of two sorts – mechanical and reflex – and that in such actions no reasoning enters at all'.[41] Citing behavioural examples of dogs, chimpanzees and orangutans, London countered that some species do have a sense of self-awareness, are capable of rudimentary reasoning and possess what he calls 'the power of choice'.[42] London's more generous estimations of animal cognition anticipate the findings of later researchers such as the primatologists Jane Goodall and Frans de Waal.

On 4 April they departed for the island of Raiatea in French Polynesia and cruised on to Bora Bora, where the Londons met a man named Tehei and his wife Bihaura. These two were exceptionally cordial hosts, and he commemorated their hospitality in *The Cruise of the Snark*, recalling

> that of all the entertainment I have received in this world at the hands of all sorts of races in all sorts of places, I have never received entertainment that equalled this at the hands of this

brown-skinned couple of Tahaa . . . I do not refer to the presents, the free handed generousness, the high abundance, but to the fineness of courtesy and consideration and tact, and to the sympathy that was real sympathy in that it was understanding. They did nothing they thought ought to be done for us, according to their standards, but they did what they divined we wanted to be done for us, while their divination was most successful. It would be impossible to enumerate the hundreds of little acts of consideration they performed during the few days of our intercourse. Let it suffice for me to say that of all hospitality and entertainment I have known, in no case was theirs not only not excelled, but in no case was it quite equalled. Perhaps the most delightful feature of it was that it was due to no training, to no complex social ideals, but that it was the untutored and spontaneous outpouring from their hearts.[43]

Tehei, a skilled sailor, joined the *Snark* crew, and they continued westwards towards American Samoa. On 29 April they anchored off of Manua, where London and Charmian were entertained by King-Tui Manu'a and Queen Vaitupu. On 2 May they arrived at Tutuila in Pago Pago harbour and on 6 May headed to Apia on the island of Upolu, where the couple stayed for the next two weeks at the plush International Hotel. While there, London paid homage to Robert Louis Stevenson, another of his literary heroes. 'Of all the stories that I have ever read,' he later wrote in 1914, 'I place Stevenson's *Treasure Island* first.'[44] The Londons and Martin Johnson traipsed up through the jungle to Stevenson's former estate in the village of Vailima to visit the author's gravesite. On 13 May London gave his 'Revolution' lecture at the Central Hotel, and the *Snark* departed from Upolu the next day for Savai'i in German Samoa.[45] Approaching the island on 16 May, the crew witnessed the spectacular eruption of one of the island's volcanoes and watched as streams of lava flowed into the sea, dripping copiously from precipices a hundred feet above the ocean. They anchored near the village of Matautu on Savai'i's north shore. Journeying inland to investigate, they were stunned by the devastation wreaked on the island's terrain and its villages by the streaming lava.

The *Snark* cruised on, passing out of the Polynesian subregion of Oceania into the Melanesian subregion and anchoring at Suva in the Fiji Islands on 27 May. They left from Suva on 6 June, sailing towards the New Hebrides islands (the present-day nation of Vanuatu) some 1,300 kilometres (800 mi.) to the southwest.[46] The *Snark* landed at Port Resolution on the island of Tanna on 11 June. Around this time, the crew was starting to suffer from 'Solomon sores', or yaws, which are caused by a spirochete bacterium that commonly infects cuts or abrasions on the skin, expanding wounds into wider and deeper ulcers. 'I was puzzled and frightened,' London groaned. 'All my life my skin had been famous for its healing powers, yet here was something that would

Jack and Charmian London on the *Snark* in Apia (Samoa), 1908.

not heal. Instead, it was daily eating up more skin, while it had eaten down clear through the skin and was eating up the muscle itself.'[47] Instead of healing, small cuts and bug bites rapidly grew into open lesions. To treat himself and some of the crew members, London applied a mercury-based corrosive sublimate directly to the wounds. He used especially high doses of the corrosive sublimate on his own sores, which almost certainly contributed to the kidney damage responsible for his death.[48] The crew was also beginning to experience various other ailments, including malaria, assorted fevers and a poison-ivy-like skin rash known locally as scratch-scratch.

The *Snark* was moving into ever-remoter territory, where cannibalism and headhunting had been traditional activities in the not-too-distant past. On Tanna, they toured the Mount Yasur volcano, where they watched volcanic eruptions fling huge boulders high in the air and out beyond the crater's edge. They also hiked inland to visit a remote tribal village in the island's jungle interior.[49] To London, these islanders appeared more savage and primitive than the indigenous populations they had previously encountered in Hawaii and on other South Sea islands. Their skin was much darker and their bodies were liberally smeared or painted with various designs, and they sported an elaborate array of body piercings. Embellished accounts of cannibalism and headhunting no doubt instilled additional insecurity and fear among the visitors. In truth, the region's indigenous populations had often been exploited, misunderstood, murdered and terrorized by European colonials. They had just cause to be wary of outsiders. London's views of the Melanesians were more negative than they had been towards Polynesians, and, at times, his attitude and language are racist. In his essay on a form of pidgin English used among traders and indigenous Melanesians, for instance, he writes that a 'common language was necessary – a language so simple that a child could learn it, with a vocabulary as limited as the intelligence of the savages upon whom it was to be used'.[50] While his perceptions of Melanesians were frequently racist, at other times he seemed to clearly grasp the injustice of colonial exploitation and sympathized with oppressed non-white populations. His Solomon stories 'Yah! Yah! Yah!' and 'Mauki' are representative examples of his ongoing colonial ambivalence.

The *Snark* arrived at Santa Ana, Port Mary, in the Solomon Islands, on 28 June 1908. The boat was almost immediately encircled by fierce-looking warriors in canoes, who seemed ready to do battle. Screaming and wielding rifles, clubs and spears, they had profusely tattooed bodies and some had wild-boar tusk nose-rings and blackened teeth filed to sharp points. Nothing escalated beyond this impressive spectacle, and the next day the Londons ended up trading peacefully with the warriors.[51] On 7 July the *Snark* arrived on the island of Guadalcanal at Penduffryn Plantation. The British owners entertained the crew with a variety of festivities that included a masquerade ball and the liberal consumption of hashish. Later, London would base the setting of his novel *Adventure* (1911) on the Penduffryn Plantation. He was sick with malaria on 12 July, and other crew members were coming down with fever as well. London was also experiencing rectal pains, which would later be diagnosed as a double fistula. Both he and Charmian were taking quinine for fevers, but they gamely agreed to accompany one Captain Jensen of the yacht *Minota* to the island of Malaita on an expedition to recruit plantation workers.

London had heard negative reports of the plantation labour recruitment practices in the Solomons, and he wanted to see the process for himself. On a recruiting trip six months before, the *Minota* had been attacked by the indigenous population, who stormed the boat and chopped its former captain to death. (When they boarded the *Minota*, the Londons could not help noticing the deep hatchet gouges on their cabin door from that attack.) The recruitment of native peoples to work on the plantations, known in the region as 'blackbirding', was a highly dubious enterprise. Many regarded it as more akin to kidnapping and slavery than contractual labour. Tellingly, the railings around the *Minota*'s decks were lined with a double row of barbed wire from bow to stern. London had made sure to bring his rifles and plenty of ammunition.

Ten days into the trip, the *Minota* had picked up some recruits at Malu and was easing through a channel in the outer reef when a sudden wind shift caused the vessel's fin keel to ground on a reef. Stuck atop the reef, the *Minota* began to be repeatedly slammed onto the hard coral by the surf. The impacts were tremendous, and the yacht's break-up seemed imminent. The indigenous islanders saw their chance and, in a flash, surrounded the *Minota* in their canoes, positioning themselves to plunder the floundering vessel as soon as an opportunity presented itself. Brandishing their rifles, the crew held the attackers off – for the moment. Desperate, London hurriedly composed a letter requesting assistance to Captain Keller of the *Eugenie*, another recruiting vessel anchored about 8 kilometres (5 mi.) away behind a bend of the island. In exchange for some tobacco, he managed to convince an islander to paddle over to the *Eugenie* and deliver the letter. The surf continued to pound the *Minota*'s hull against the reef as the hours passed. Amazingly, the boat held together. They jettisoned all the extra weight they could remove – even tossing pig iron from the ballast overboard, but the boat still wouldn't budge. Poised to ransack *Minota*, the islanders patiently floated nearby. Finally, a whale boat from the *Eugenie* under a huge sail burst through a rain squall with Captain Keller at the helm, revolver in belt, accompanied by a heavily armed crew. The *Minota* and its crew were saved from the islanders, but it took three days to pull the boat off the reef.[52]

After the escapade on the *Minota*, the *Snark* coasted to Meringe Lagoon on Santa Isabel, where they stayed for seventeen days. Everyone aboard was still dealing with yaws and fever. The *Snark* sailed 320 kilometres (200 mi.) to Lord Howe Atoll and then on to Tasman Atoll, and by 15 October they were back in Guadalcanal.

The rashes, fevers and yaws continued to torment the crew. The *Snark* was becoming a hospital ship, and it probably didn't help that the boat was rife with centipedes and cockroaches. London had been bitten twice by 15-centimetre (6 in.) centipedes while sleeping.[53] His assortment of ailments was expanding and worsening. He began to think he might have leprosy when his skin developed a silvery hue and his hands swelled painfully and the skin began to peel off in multiple layers. By early October the Londons, along with Martin Johnson, decided to take a steamer to Sydney, Australia to get medical treatment. There, on 30 November, doctors operated successfully on London's double fistula but were unable to diagnose the ailments that were afflicting his hands and joints. He spent five weeks in the hospital. Describing his ailing hands, London wrote:

> The mysterious malady that affected my hands was too much for the Australian specialists . . . It extended from my hands to my feet so that at times I was helpless as a child. On occasion my hands were twice their natural size, with seven dead and dying layers skins peeling off at the same time. There were times when my toe-nails, in twenty-four hours, grew as thick as they were long. After filing them off, inside another twenty-four hours they were as thick as before.[54]

The peeling skin on his hands was most likely produced by handling, without gloves, the corrosive sublimate used to treat yaws. Recently, Frank Praetorius has made a convincing case that London's symptoms – skin rash and transient arthritis in the extremities – were caused by the mosquito-borne virus endemic to the region that causes what is now called Ross River Disease, *Epidemic polyarthritis*. Given that the symptoms of Ross River

Disease last about six months and then disappear, Praetorius posits that London was infected with the disease before the passage to Lord Howe on 8 September 1908.[55]

Citing his ill health, London cancelled the *Snark* cruise on 8 December. On 9 January 1909 the Londons went on a month-long recuperative trip to Tasmania, and on 8 April they took passage, with Nakata, on the collier *Tymeric* to Ecuador, during which London's health improved markedly. They stayed in Ecuador for a month and visited Quito, where they climbed 3,660 metres (12,000 ft) up Mount Chimborazo. London took in a bullfight. He was not a fan, but the experience did inspire his story 'The Madness of John Harned'. They boarded the steamship *Erica* and arrived in Panama on 25 June, where they went alligator hunting on the River Guayas and viewed the construction work on the Panama Canal. By 7 July they were on the *Turriabla* bound for New Orleans. They took a train to the Grand Canyon for some quick sightseeing and were back in Oakland on 21 July. London was ready to get back to his mild California climate and do some ranching.

# 8

# Back to the Land: Beauty Ranch and California (1909–12)

I believe the soil is our one indestructible asset . . .
Jack London[1]

Sometimes it seems to me that all the world, all life, everything, had taken up residence inside of me and was clamoring for me to be the spokesman.
Jack London[2]

During the *Snark* cruise, Macmillan had published three books by London: a collection of stories, *Love of Life* (1907), his tramping memoir *The Road* (1907) and his socialist-dystopian novel *The Iron Heel* (1908). His literary production had been unflagging throughout the voyage: he had completed 22 short stories, most of *The Cruise of the Snark* (1911) and two novels – *Martin Eden* (1909) and *Adventure* (1911). After the journey's end he had written several non-fiction pieces while still in Australia and reported on the Burns–Johnson boxing match that took place in Sydney. In addition to beginning work on his novel *Burning Daylight* (1910) on his way back to California, he also finished five more stories, including three of his most eminent: 'South of the Slot', 'Samuel' and 'A Piece of Steak'. By the time he returned to California in late July 1909, the 33-year-old author had published eight novels, seven collections of short stories, one memoir, one play, one collection of political essays and a book-length sociological exposé, as well as co-authoring, with Anna Strunsky, *The Kempton-Wace Letters*.

That summer in Glen Ellen London was happy to be back on Beauty Ranch and in the temperate California climate. When he had bought the first parcel of the ranch in 1905, he described it as '130 acres of the most beautiful, primitive land to be found anywhere in California':

> There are great redwoods on it, some of them thousands of years old – in fact, the redwoods are as fine and magnificent as any to be found anywhere outside the tourist groves. Also there are great firs, tan-tan bark oaks, maples, live oaks, white oaks, black oaks, mandrono and manzanita galore. There are canyons, several streams of water, many springs, etc., etc. In fact, it is impossible to really describe the place. All I can say is this – I have been all over California off and on all my life, for the last two months I have been riding all over these hills, looking for just such a place, and I must say that I have never seen anything like it.[3]

He was now ready to dive into the cultivation and development of the property. Amid his other writings and travels over the next seven years, the ranch would be a consuming interest, as he continued to enhance, refine and expand its operations. The full 1,400-acre (570 ha) Beauty Ranch was made up of seven smaller land holdings that he was able to buy and consolidate over the years. First, in 1905, he bought the 130-acre (53 ha) Hill Ranch. While London was away on the *Snark*, Ninetta Eames had overseen the purchase of the 127-acre (51 ha) La Motte Ranch as well as the 24-acre (10 ha) Caroline Kohler Ranch in 1909. London acquired the 9-acre (4 ha) Fish Ranch the same year and the 700-acre (283 ha) Kohler & Frohling Ranch in 1910. The Kohler & Frohling winery buildings on 12 acres (5 ha)

Jack London at the reins of a horse-drawn hay wagon on Beauty Ranch, 1916.

were obtained in 1911, and, finally, he added the 400 acres (162 ha) of Freund Ranch in 1913.[4] As with his intellectual and literary efforts to blend contrasting ideas into higher philosophical syntheses, he approached farming and ranching with a similar kind of fusional vision. He declared, 'I see my farm in terms of the world, and I see the world in terms of my farm.'[5] The plan was to harness the full fecundity of the 'primitive' land through the application of the latest advances in scientific farming techniques, livestock breeding, land terracing (as he had seen practised in Korea), crop rotation, organic fertilizers and various labour-saving designs and techniques. His progressive agricultural strategies were important precursors to later developments in organic farming and environmental sustainability. London did not want to be a mere 'gentleman farmer'. His was a grand, holistic and restorative enterprise. He declared,

> I am rebuilding worn-out hillside lands that were worked out and destroyed by our wasteful California pioneer farmers. I am not using commercial fertilizer. I believe the soil is our one indestructible asset, and by green manures,

> nitrogen-gathering cover crops, animal manure, rotation
> of crops, proper tillage and draining, I am getting results
> which the Chinese have demonstrated for forty centuries.[6]

He cultivated successful harvests of hay, alfalfa, grapes, corn and prunes. He also bred cattle, goats, horses, pigs and sheep. Ranch expenses were considerable and ever on the increase, but London's unabated literary output continued to keep pace, if at times just barely, with expenditures. He suffered setbacks with crop failures and livestock deaths, while the market never materialized for the 150,000 eucalyptus trees he had planted on the ranch. His ultimate goal, though, was 'to leave the land better for my having been'.[7] In 1910 London hired his stepsister Eliza as ranch superintendent. Along with her son Irving, she moved to the ranch in 1911, and was a dependable and trusted supervisor who oversaw various undertakings and construction projects. Though he died before he could fully realize his lofty ambitions for the property, London hoped that he could one day make Beauty Ranch into a commune that would support thirty or forty families and have its own schoolhouse, store and post office.[8]

During this time London was also fending off charges of plagiarism that had emerged in July. The indictment was levelled by writer Frank Harris, whose 1901 article 'The Bishop of London and Public Morality' had been used by London as the basis for a speech delivered by a character named Bishop Morehouse in Chapter Seven of *The Iron Heel*. London freely admitted to copying the speech from Harris's article, which he had apparently read as an authentic transcription of a talk given by the Bishop of London. The problem was that Harris's piece was not an actual speech by the bishop, but his own satirical lampoon that highlighted the bishop's hypocrisy. London maintained: 'I took what I saw in the newspaper as the quoted words of what the Bishop of London had actually uttered on a public platform . . . The laugh is on me. I confess to having been fooled by Mr Harris's canard.'[9] It wasn't the first time he had been accused of plagiarism. He was cited for importing elements of Egerton R. Young's *My Dogs in the Northland* into *The Call of the Wild*; his story 'Love of Life' was singled out for reusing a true-life account of a man lost in the wilderness from the article 'Lost in the Land of the Midnight Sun' by Augustus Bridle and J. K. MacDonald; and he was criticised for replicating elements of Stanley Waterloo's novel *The Story of Ab* in his novel *Before Adam*. In all three instances, London acknowledged that he had used the specified works as references, but he adamantly maintained that he had sufficiently transformed the sources in ways that rightly distinguished his creative work as his own. Young's book, London groused, 'was a narrative of fact' and that 'fiction-writers have always considered actual experiences of life to be a lawful field for exploitation'.[10] Similarly, in the case of 'Lost in the Land of the Midnight Sun', he maintained: 'It is common practice of authors to draw material for their stories from newspapers . . . So common is this practice of authors that it is recommended by all instructors in the art of the short story.'[11] And regarding resemblances between *Before Adam* and Waterloo's *The Story of Ab*, he protested: 'I wrote *Before Adam* as a reply to the *Story of Ab*, because I considered the latter unscientific . . . Also, I tried to reproduce the primitive world in an artistic form, which same Mr. Waterloo did not do.'[12] London did emboss borrowed materials with his own artistic elaborations. He was a compelling storyteller whose work was thematically dynamic, but he was not as adept at inventing wholly unique character types or devising innovative plot structures. In the eyes of most scholars, his literary remixing exonerates him from outright plagiarism, but throughout his career he was constantly trolling for fresh plots and regularly appropriated ideas and scenarios from a variety of sources (non-fiction of all stripes, old myths and fables, magazine and newspaper articles, and stories he had heard). He even purchased plot scenarios from writer Sinclair Lewis. As long as he infused the source with some degree of imaginative flair or artistically refashioned its details towards his own narrative ends, he felt justified in repurposing the work of others towards his own creative design.

As London implemented improvements on the ranch following the *Snark* cruise, he was working on *Burning Daylight*, a novel that features depictions of California farmsteading. Over the years, *Burning Daylight* has garnered less critical attention than his previous novel, *Martin Eden*, which had been published in September 1909. Read in tandem, however, these two works reveal London's mixed assessments of human agency.

*Martin Eden* is his most modernistic novel and focuses on subjects including alienation, depression, mass media and celebrity. This work traces the self-education, rise to prominence, disillusionment and suicide of its eponymous hero. Martin Eden starts out as a sensitive but uneducated sailor and ends up as a famous but depressed author who commits suicide. In the book's opening chapters, Martin falls in love with the beautiful and ethereal Ruth Morse, who seems to epitomize all the social refinement and intellectual richness of the socially well-to-do classes. Deeply enamoured of Ruth and enchanted by her posh upper-middle-class life, Martin is determined to make her class and her lifestyle his own, and soon hits on the idea of becoming an author and writing his way to a socio-economic status worthy of Ruth. London details the intense course of Martin's teeming intellectual odyssey as he passionately reads, studies and writes. For most readers, London's depiction of the enthusiasm with which Martin commits himself to writing and his self-education constitute the novel's most enthralling episodes. It is also loosely semi-biographical. Ruth and the Morse household are based mostly on Mabel Applegarth and her family.

Extraordinarily self-motivated, Martin persists at the writing game and continues to develop intellectually and creatively, but publishers keep rejecting his submissions. He grows more cynical and begins to see that Ruth's apparent sophistication is only a veneer masking her deeply engrained conventionality. He does find a kindred spirit in the tubercular aesthete poet Russ Brissenden, based partially on London's friend George Sterling, who admonishes Martin that he should 'love beauty for its own sake' and ignore the vicissitudes of the literary marketplace.[13] He also tells him to forget about Ruth, whom Brissenden misogynistically derides as a 'pusillanimous product of bourgeois-sheltered life'.[14] Brissenden commits suicide and Ruth dumps Martin, but then the tide abruptly turns on Martin's literary career. His works are published to great acclaim, and he is hailed by formerly indifferent associates and feted by the upper classes. Seemingly, his hard work and perseverance have paid off. Martin becomes a celebrity and a cultural sensation, while editors commence celebrating the very works they previously snubbed. But a profound disenchantment has already seized his psyche. The hypocrisy, venality and hollowness of his sudden celebrity fracture Martin's sense of self beyond recovery. He laments to himself: 'Martin Eden, the famous writer did not exist! Martin Eden, the famous writer was a vapor that had arisen in the mob-mind and by the mob-mind had been thrust into the corporeal being of Mart Eden, the hoodlum and sailor.'[15] Fame has reified his being into 'a purely fictitious value' and he descends into a state of nihilistic depression: 'I am a sick man – oh, not my body. It is my soul, my brain. I seem to have lost all values. I care for nothing.'[16] Alas, he cannot run order through the chaos of his shattered identity. Ruth attempts to reunite with Martin, offering herself in 'free love', but he remains emotionally apathetic.[17] He eventually chooses suicide. In transit to the South Seas, he slides out of a steamship porthole and forcibly drowns himself in the deeps of the Pacific. Denying and sneering at his own 'will to live', he proclaims that he, too, 'had will, – ay, will strong enough that with one last exertion it could destroy itself and cease to be'.[18] He dives down, 'compell[ing] his arms and legs to drive him deeper', until the air is driven 'from his lungs in a great explosive rush'.[19]

Disastrous as well for Martin had been his devotion to the ideal of upward mobility, which enshrines the twin objectives of social ascent and monetary success as life's *summum bonum*. Martin's thwarted idealism, coupled with his falsely naive perceptions of Ruth and society, are the primary reasons for his disillusionment, but, as evidenced even in his suicide, Martin stands out as one of London's most conspicuously self-determining human characters.

Throughout the novel he acts independently, defies class boundaries and overcomes educational and cultural disadvantages. In a distinctly existential manner, Martin creates himself, and, in the end, he deliberately kills himself. His drive and determination, though, cannot remedy the psychological deracination wrought by the modern maladies of dislocation and estrangement. As evidenced in Martin's despair, the fluid intangibility of modernity's ills only renders his condition more difficult to diagnose and remedy. Some readers have found London's depiction of Martin's suicide problematic, complaining that it occurs too abruptly and unexpectedly. But in addition to revealing the capricious psycho-emotional effects of modernity, the portrayal of Martin's self-annihilation credibly advances the uncomfortable reality that suicide often eludes rational explanation and tends to generate more questions than it answers.

Whereas London depicts Martin's suicide as a supreme act of the will, *Burning Daylight* is a work in which notions of agency are notably muted. After *Martin Eden*, with its modern themes of subjectivity and discontinuity, it may seem odd that London would re-engage with the more naturalistic ideas that he had explored early on in his career, but he often revisited former themes and ideas from alternative perspectives – *The Call of the Wild* and *White Fang* being the most prominent example of the practice. Similarly, *Martin Eden* and *Burning Daylight* form another literary diptych in which London offers an extended meditation on the problems of free will and determinism. Together these two novels present duelling ironies in regard to the scope and constraints of human freedom. Ironically, the confirmations of human autonomy depicted in *Martin Eden* only lead to negative outcomes, while, conversely, the lack of agency portrayed in *Burning Daylight* has positive consequences.

Because of its happy ending and bounty of dramatic action and romance, *Burning Daylight* is not usually considered one of London's major novels. The book, however, offers an intriguingly complex deterministic portrait of its protagonist, as it chronicles the success, degeneration and rejuvenation of the Klondike miner, entrepreneur and rancher Elam Harnish – nicknamed Burning Daylight. After making his initial fortune in the Northland, Daylight moves to California and becomes an elite but jaded (and alcohol-dependent) financier. Then, after falling in love and marrying his progressive-thinking and beautifully athletic secretary, Dede Mason, he abandons his wealth to lead a serene, low-impact life in the country with his new bride. Although Daylight possesses a capacity for dominance that marks him as 'The King of the Klondike' in the Northland and as a successful financial tycoon back in California, London presents him as one whose actions, vigorous and large as they may be, are merely the outcomes of his genetically programmed temperament and environmental determinants.[20] London's depiction consistently renders Daylight's actions as mere consequences of a combination of inner drives and exterior influences, which persistently push, pull and reshape him. The first chapter establishes the novel's deterministic orientation in terms of extrinsic pressures: '[Daylight] was a man's man primarily, and the instinct in him to play the game of life was strong. Environment had determined what form that game should take . . . Pluck and endurance counted in the game, but the great god Chance dealt the cards.'[21] Further diminishing Daylight's autonomy, the narrator is the explanation that his amazing physical constitution is an indiscriminately generated physiological consequence – that is, a biological determinate – of the 'supreme organic excellence residing in the stuff of the muscles themselves.'[22] And his 'almost perfect brain and muscular coordination . . . was simple, in its way, and no virtue of his. He had been born with this endowment . . . He was so made. His muscles were high power explosives. The levers of his body snapped into play like the jaws of steel traps.'[23] Additionally, the novel's three main settings – the Northland, San Francisco and the California countryside – establish the environment as a decisive shaping influence. While the Northland evokes salubrious ambition and camaraderie, San Francisco's rapacious corporate culture has a degenerative effect on Daylight's character. The influence of the 'modern supermen' capitalists in the novel's middle chapters, who 'preach a code of right and wrong to their victims which they themselves [do] not practise', degrades Daylight's morality.[24] He loses his 'old-time, whole-souled geniality' and becomes 'cynical, bitter, and brutal'.[25] Daylight comes to realize: 'Cities did not make for comradeship as did the Alaskan trail.'[26] The scale of the urban marketplace, its increasing complexity, intensity and corruption, become all consuming, and Daylight can only find reprieve through the deadening effects of alcohol, initiating a plot of decline that sets in near the midpoint of the novel. Urban commerce corrodes Daylight's optimism and enfeebles his muscles. He becomes a 'money slave with a whiskey-rotted carcass',[27] and the city life 'dry-rot[s] his muscles with alcohol'.[28]

Daylight's secretary and love interest, the robustly feminine Dede Mason, diagnoses his 'disease of business'.[29] She chides Daylight: 'Your money destroys you . . . You, a man of the open, have been cooping yourself up in the cities with all that that means. You are not the same man at all and your money is destroying you . . . You have become harsh and cruel . . . Your money and the life it compels you to lead have done all this.'[30]

Crucially, Dede also awakens Daylight's libidinal desires and she – another exterior force – curbs his degenerative descent and becomes his primary regenerative influence. As their romantic relationship deepens, the effects of her anti-corporate attitudes, in conjunction with her arousal of Daylight's sexual desires, become the influences that determine Daylight's actions in the last quarter of the novel. Previously, Daylight escaped love 'just as he had escaped smallpox'.[31] But when Dede finally enters his life: 'Luck had dealt [Daylight] the most remarkable card in the deck . . . Love was the card, and it beat them all.'[32] When Dede's sexual allure prompts Daylight to give up the hard-drinking business life, a positive mania replaces a negative one. Besotted, he complies with Dede's demand that, to have her, he must give up business for marriage: 'I've taken your preaching to heart, and I've come to the penitent form. You are my Lord God, and I'm sure going to serve you.'[33]

Thus compelled, Daylight abandons the city and finance, and the couple move to the country to run a modest Sonoma ranch. Daylight's adoption of a simplified agrarian life is decidedly more determined than chosen. Settled on the ranch, he tells Dede: 'Little woman . . . you're sure responsible for it all.'[34] And he no longer needs to succumb to a desire for alcohol when 'the thought of her was like a cocktail'.[35] Daylight soon discovers rich gold deposits on the ranch, an occurrence that typically signals an irresistible temptation in naturalistic novels, but he reburies the gold and returns to the couple's modest cottage. His rejection may seem to indicate an agency that defies the novel's deterministic design, but here at the narrative's close, London is again depicting how environmental forces and inner drives persist in directing Daylight's actions; for, in this instance, the instinct-driven need to maintain his romantic-sexual union with Dede in the pastoral Valley of the Moon is merely more powerful than his desire for money.

As London was writing *Burning Daylight*, Charmian became pregnant during late September or early October 1909. The couple was elated. He was pining for a son, but professed not to care if it was a boy or girl. If the baby was a boy, he would be named Mate. If a girl, her name would be Joy. On 19 June 1910 Charmian gave birth to an apparently healthy baby girl. Tragically the infant's spine was severely damaged during the delivery, and Joy died 38 hours after the birth. For a time, Charmian's life was also in peril. She had gone into shock after her placenta failed to deliver. She recovered but the couple was devastated over the loss of Joy. Charmian's physical recuperation would last through the first part of August, and London found himself embroiled in a nasty bar-room brawl in the immediate aftermath of his daughter's death.

In the hours following Joy's passing, a distraught London wandered through Oakland's Tenderloin district and along some of his old haunts on 7th Street. Under his arm were several copies of the autobiography of the boxer Jim Jeffries. Jeffries was scheduled to fight Jack Johnson in the upcoming World Heavyweight Boxing Championship and London, who was under contract with the *New York Herald* to cover the fight, had purchased several extra copies for his reporter buddies. When he entered the Tavern Cafe and walked towards the toilets, he was suddenly attacked by the manager, Tim Muldowney, who apparently thought London was 'a quack doctor bent on posting some placards' in the tavern.[36] London tried to avoid the confrontation, but was shoved around and punched by Muldowney and his cronies, who would not relent. He finally dodged his way into the street and informed the police that he had been assaulted, but Muldowney – backed by his patrons – denied the accusation, claiming that London had come in drunk and assaulted him. London ended up being arrested. He was incensed by the turn of events, and the press sensationalized the incident. He brought counter charges against Muldowney. When Judge George Samuels eventually dismissed the case on 8 July, giving each man the 'benefit of the doubt', London grew more outraged and vowed legal revenge.[37] Eventually, he discovered that Judge Samuels owned a property share in Muldowney's tavern, and exposed the connection to the press. Samuels was not re-elected.[38] The protracted episode showed London's prominent righteous streak and his obsessiveness.

In the midst of this fracas, and with Charmian's encouragement, London travelled to Reno, Nevada, on 23 June to honour his commitment with the *Herald* to report on the Jack Johnson–Jim Jeffries World Championship Boxing bout. Heralded as the fight of the century, the contest was widely seen as a racial showdown – a white-versus-black battle. While in Sydney, Australia, in December 1908, London had seen the African American Johnson soundly defeat Tommy Burns for the title. Shortly afterwards, a call had gone out for a 'Great White Hope' to emerge and retake the title. Former Heavyweight Champion Jim Jeffries, a white fighter, came out of retirement to challenge Johnson. Jeffries was taciturn and gruff, while Johnson was flashy and gregarious. One of the greatest boxers of all time, Johnson had more than enough talent and skill to back up his flamboyance – and London admired his verbal

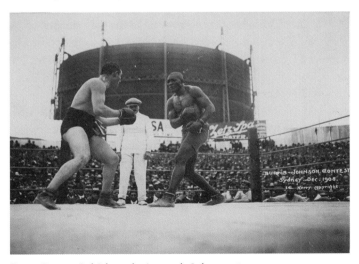

Tommy Burns vs. Jack Johnson boxing match, Sydney, 1908.

wit, in and out of the ring. In his articles leading up to the fight London makes no bones about the fact that he personally wanted Jeffries to win, but he enjoyed spending time in Johnson's camp and was charmed by the boxer's defiant, over-the-top personality.[39] Conversely, he found Jeffries's brusqueness demeaning. Still, he pulled for Jeffries during the fight, but the 'White Hope' was plainly outmatched. It was clear to London that Johnson was the superior boxer and his coverage duly recorded that Johnson dominated the fight. 'In the fiddling of those first rounds,' London reported, 'the honors lay with Johnson, and for the rounds after the seventh or eighth it was more Johnson, while for the closing rounds it was all Johnson.'[40] The white press overwhelmingly tried to downplay Johnson's victory, but London lauded the champion, declaring in his dispatch on the fight: 'Johnson is a wonder.'[41]

In the autumn of 1910 London bought the *Roamer*, a 9-metre (30 ft) yawl perfect for extended sailing trips in the northern California bay and inland waters. He paid $175 dollars for the boat, which had a wide beam, a spacious cabin and large sails. 'Once a sailor, always a sailor,' proclaimed London. 'The savour of the salt never stales. The sailor never grows so old that he does not care to go back for one more wresting bout with wind and wave.'[42] He and Charmian took off on a month-long cruise in the middle of October and met up with friends from the old days, Charley Le Grant of the Fish Patrol and old French Frank from London's waterfront days. It was the first of many prolonged cruises on the *Roamer*, which served as a comfy getaway over the next few years. Though he was rarely at ease for long, London could relax on the *Roamer*. As Charmian later recalled: 'The vessel all in order, laid against a river-bank for the night, he would sit, placidly smoking in the blue dungarees and old tam, humped comfortably on deck, his soft-shod feet hanging over the rail, line overboard for cat-fish or black bass.'[43]

Ready for new adventure closer to home, from 12 June to 5 September 1911 London, Charmian and their valet Nakata set

Jack and Charmian London, along with Nakata, riding in a horse-drawn carriage, near Eureka, California, 1911.

out on a 2,400-kilometre (1,500 mi.) trip in a four-horse wagon up through northern California and into Oregon. As London explained: 'Having selected Sonoma Valley for our abiding place, Charmian and I decided it was about time we knew what we had in our own county and the neighbouring ones.'[44] It was another all-encompassing venture. London would write in the mornings while Charmian typed his manuscripts, and he would drive the wagon through the afternoons. But they weren't completely roughing it on this go-around. Each night – instead of camping – they stayed in hotels and would usually hit the road again the next day after their morning work and breakfast. Compared to the *Snark* voyage, this was a more leisurely undertaking. At times, the roads could be dusty and rough, but for the most part, the going was easy and the weather was temperate.

During this period, Charmian wrote that 'Jack was living so fully – a life balanced with essential interest and endeavor and simplest of amusements. The test, I am sure, he undertook deliberately. To him relaxation consisted not in cessation but in change of thought and occupation.'[45] Travel, horses, farming, sailing, politics, friends, entertaining, whisky and wine – he sought to embrace it all. His reading also continued to range widely across the humanities and sciences, from contemporary newspapers and farming reports, to Greek philosophers, psychoanalysis and Norse mythology. Along with Charmian, the one constant was his writing, and though he continued writing Northland stories, his work from 1910 onwards was engaging increasingly diverse subjects and themes. *The Scarlet Plague* is a post-apocalyptic novella that depicts how a handful of human survivors from a global pandemic struggle to adapt to a re-primitivized California landscape. In 'The Mexican', his Latino protagonist is a socialist revolutionary-cum-boxer who fights gamely for the cause. 'War' is the story of an American Civil War cavalry scout and is an aesthetic gem of poignancy and understatement. 'Told in the Drooling Ward' delivers unexpected and politically charged insights through the perspective of an intellectually disabled narrator. And 'The Night-born' follows a defiant female adventurer who abandons her abusive husband to live a life on her own terms in the Northland wilderness.

On 5 September 1911 the couple moved to a renovated cottage on Beauty Ranch near the old Kohler-Frohling Winery. The Londons were hospitable and welcoming hosts on the ranch, but whether at home or travelling, they rarely deviated from the work schedules. London printed a memo informing visitors of daily activities: 'We rise early, and work into the forenoon. Therefore, we do not see our guests until afternoons and evenings. You may breakfast from 7 till 9, and then we all get together for dinner at 12:30. You will find this a good place to work, if you have work to do. Or if you prefer to play, there are horses, saddles, and rigs. In the summer we have a swimming pool.'[46]

Settling in and taking some time off from travel, the Londons spent their longest period in continuous residence on Beauty Ranch during the four months from September 1911 to the end of the year.[47] London typically rose early in the mornings around 5 a.m. and wrote for about three hours. Then he worked on revising his

Jack London horseback riding on Beauty Ranch, *c.* 1910.

galleys and typescripts. Next, he would attend to his correspondence and read the newspapers until 12.30, when he would join guests for 'dinner', their main meal of the day. After dinner, he might attend to one or two ranch or business matters, but the afternoons were primarily spent having fun – horseback riding, flying kites, boxing, swimming and so on. In the evenings, he mingled with guests for drinks and had supper. They played cards, conversed and debated, listened to music on the phonograph, gave literary readings and Charmian often played the piano. He would withdraw to his bedroom at around 10.30 p.m. Normally, he read and took notes deep into the night, usually falling asleep sometime after midnight. In their cottage on the ranch, he and Charmian slept in separate rooms due to his late nights and her frequent bouts of insomnia.

By his bedside Nakata made sure that London had an abundant supply of cigarettes and that his special brass Korean ashtray was ever at the ready. Nakata also laid out snacks of fruit and dried fish and neatly arranged London's notepads and freshly sharpened pencils. Placed in close reach were his most recent galleys and various files, along with newspapers and magazines arranged by date with the most recent issues on top. And, as Charmian recalls,

> there were no less than three bottles of liquid of one sort or another. For Jack always maintained that it was a mercy, with his almost uninterrupted smoking, the alcohol he consumed, and certain sedentary spells when he took little exercise, that he 'breathed through the skin' – by which he meant free perspiring. Therefore he drank almost excessive quantities of . . . grapejuice, buttermilk, and endless draughts of water.[48]

London led an intense but unhealthy life, and by the end of 1911, he was likely already feeling the effects of the kidney disease that would eventually lead to his demise.

In January 1912 the couple, along with Nakata, travelled to New York City for a two-month stay, mainly because London wanted to explore new publishing opportunities with firms other than Macmillan. The problem was that London had flooded the market with short-story collections, and he did not want to bring out his new volumes as incrementally as George Brett at Macmillan desired. London never broke with Macmillan, but Brett agreed to release him from the exclusivity clause in their contract so that he could publish with other firms. The trip was packed with business meetings and much socializing and partying. Heavy drinking, poker games and late nights out became routine for London in the big city. His carousing placed a serious burden on his marriage. The trip did have a few good moments for the couple. They had happy visits with several friends, including with Anna Strunsky, now a mother and married to William English Walling, a wealthy socialist and labour reformer. They also attended plays, dinners and meetings with fellow socialists. But Charmian, who did not drink, complained that 'the city reached into [London] and plucked to light the least admirable of his qualities'.[49] 'With Jack's wife,' friend Joseph Noel remarked of the couple's travails in New York, 'it was the problem of an incorrigible husband toward whom she felt all the responsibility of a mother toward a wayward son.'[50] London knew his indulgences were destructive but, for him, the city's sybaritic abundance made moderation all but impossible. Even though his self-centredness and hedonistic abandon were the root issues, he projected his dismay onto the city, describing New York as a 'wild maelstrom with which the city of Rome in its wildest days could not compare'.[51] 'Great Scott, no, no!' he boomed. 'I must have the open, the big open. No big city for me, and above all not New York. I think it is the cocksure feeling of superiority which the people of the metropolis feel over the rest of the country that makes me rage.'[52] Charmian was justifiably feeling forsaken, and London was growing restive. They needed to get away.

Finally, at the end of February 1912, the couple left behind the debauchery and emotional strain of the city and headed to Baltimore to embark on another great adventure. They had decided to take the long way home and booked passage aboard the *Dirigo* to sail south around Cape Horn and back up north to Seattle, Washington.

9

# Cosmos Mariner: Final Travels and Last Days (1912–16)

I would rather be ashes than dust!
I would rather that my spark should burn out
in a brilliant blaze than it should be stifled by dry-rot.
Jack London[1]

He said that the wolf is a being of great order and that it knows what men do not: that there is no order in the world save that which death has put there.
Cormac McCarthy[2]

On 2 March 1912 Jack and Charmian London set sail out of Baltimore on the windjammer *Dirigo*. They were accompanied by their valet, Nakata, and a newly acquired puppy, a feisty little fox terrier named Possum. The *Dirigo* would take them on a 148-day, 22,500-kilometre (14,000-mi.) journey around the southern tip of South America and its treacherous Cape Horn, and then back north to Seattle, Washington. The massive 100-metre (330 ft) vessel had a steel hull and weighed 3,000 tonnes. A picturesque four-masted, square-rigged merchant sailing ship, it was one of the last of its kind, and the Londons were eager to embark on this rare odyssey that would last nearly five months. They paid $1,000 for the journey and had to sign on nominally as crew to gain passage on the *Dirigo*: London as third mate, Charmian as 'stewardess' and Nakata as cabin boy. Happily, the trip worked to rejuvenate the couple's romantic relationship and was professionally productive as well. Away from the enticements of the city and the distractions of celebrity life, the couple spent some much-needed time alone together, reading to each other, boxing, playing with Possum and climbing the *Dirigo*'s tall masts. Away from the press, parties and their usual commitments, their intimacy flourished. And it certainly helped that London swore off alcohol for the duration of the voyage. Charmian mused in her diary, 'I wonder if many wedded pairs "travel in pairs" as we do, after six years of being together . . . We don't envy any landlubber! [This voyage] is all . . . we love – this roving sailor-rush life together. It is in our veins, in our marrow; and we love it and each other's predilection for such life.'[3] The *Dirigo* trip gave the couple the time and space necessary to revitalize and deepen their emotional commitment to one another. Towards the end of May, the couple decided to '"send" for another baby' and Charmian was able to become pregnant.[4]

Nautical life, as usual, primed London's literary production. He made notes for his memoir *John Barleycorn*, and seafaring on the *Dirigo* significantly shaped his novel *The Mutiny of the Elsinore*, published in 1914. He worked steadily on his long novel, *The Valley of the Moon*, which he had begun back in the first week of December 1911, finishing it on 17 July, nine days before the *Dirigo* landed in Seattle.

The first half of *The Valley of the Moon* details the courtship and marriage of a working-class couple, along with their toils and tribulations in industrial Oakland. Saxon Brown Roberts is a laundry worker, and her husband, Billy Roberts, is a teamster and occasional professional boxer. In the city they are subjected to the brutalities of labour struggles and violent strikes. Saxon suffers a miscarriage when she is caught up in a workers' riot, and strained circumstances lead to Billy serving time in prison. Their difficulties prompt the couple to abandon the city and travel throughout rural California in search of a better life. London extols the virtues of the countryside over the strife of the city, but his pastoral inclination is more than a mere idyllic escape. Thematically, the novel is governed by an agrarian back-to-the-land motif, through which London cautions against soil depletion and orients readers towards the advantages of more sustainable agricultural practices. As Saxon and Billy proceed on their pilgrimage, they absorb the counsel and warnings from experienced farmers. They also learn about the successful agricultural methods of immigrant groups. These are mainly farmers of Portuguese, Italian, Chinese and Japanese ancestry who, in contrast to their Anglo-American counterparts, do not 'skin the soil and move, skin the soil and move'.[5] Near Carmel, the couple meet the poet-farmer Mark Hall, who links the American penchant for unsustainable farming practices to the nation's maniacal free marketeering, which he sardonically deems a 'gambler's paradise'. In a sweeping denunciation of American greed, he declares:

> When you think of the glorious chance . . . A new country, bounded by the oceans, situated just right in latitude, with the richest land and vastest natural resources of any country in the world, settled by immigrants who had thrown off all the leading strings of the Old World and were in the humor for democracy. There was only one thing to stop them from perfecting the democracy they started, and that thing was greediness.
>
> They started gobbling everything in sight like a lot of swine, and while they gobbled democracy went to smash. Gobbling became gambling . . . They moved over the face of the land like so many locusts. They destroyed everything – the Indians, the soil, the forests, just as they destroyed the buffalo and the passenger pigeon. Their morality in business and politics was gambler morality. Their laws were gambling laws . . . So they

Picture postcard featuring a view of the *Dirigo* at sea, 1912.

gobbled and gambled from the Atlantic to the Pacific, until
they'd swined a whole continent. When they'd finished with
the lands and forests and mines, they turned back, gambling
for any little stakes they'd overlooked, gambling for franchises
and monopolies, using politics to protect their crooked deals
and brace games. And democracy gone clean to smash.[6]

Mark Hall is a fictionalized version of London himself and
functions mostly, like many of the narrative's minor characters,
to advance the author's progressive agrarian agenda. For most
of the novel, however, the narrative centres on Saxon, and she is
the most fully developed female character in London's oeuvre.
Outlining his plans for the book, he wrote to his editor George
Brett: 'The woman gets the vision. She is the guiding force.'[7]
Where Billy is often pugnacious, impetuous and xenophobic,
Saxon remains composed, reasonable and more open-minded.
They eventually settle on a modest farm in Sonoma Valley and
Saxon becomes pregnant again. But the book ends ambiguously,
with Billy entertaining entrepreneurial visions of clay mining and

commercial development. It is unclear whether or not he himself will eventually succumb to the profit-making temptations of the 'gambler's paradise'.

After the *Dirigo* voyage, the couple was back on Beauty Ranch in early August when Charmian miscarried on the eleventh.[8] She had to undergo surgery to repair the damage wrought by the miscarriage, and it was not until 26 November that she was well enough to take a month-long cruise on the *Roamer* with her husband, their friend Laurie Godfrey-Smith and Possum.

By now London was well into the writing of *John Barleycorn*. Subtitled 'alcoholic memoirs', the book recounts London's lifelong struggles with alcohol and its deleterious psychological effects. The narrative is an addiction memoir in the tradition of Thomas De Quincey's *Confessions of an English Opium-eater*, and a precursor of works such as F. Scott Fitzgerald's 'The Crack-up'. As to the book's veracity, he maintained, 'I shall not go so far as to say that *John Barleycorn* is the story of my life, but I will go so far as to say that it is the true story of that part of my life.'[9] He also claimed that the book was a 'straight, true narrative of my personal experiences, and it is toned down, not up'.[10] Scholars rightly shy away from accepting the book as a factually precise autobiography. The narrative is based more on fact than fiction, but London's version of 'Jack London' is, of course, subject to the fluid alchemy of memory and the author's energetic imagination.

Thematically, *John Barleycorn* has a little something for everyone. For the sober minded, it serves as pro-prohibition propaganda and as a tract for women's suffrage. If females could get the vote, London believed, they would tip the scales in favour of prohibition. The *Rochester Union* declared the book to be the most powerful temperance argument of all time, and the Prohibition Party even nominated London for president of the United States.[11] For denial seekers, alcoholic rationalizations permeate the text. London recognizes his dependency on drink, but resolves only to moderate his future drinking. Having read *John Barleycorn* more carefully than most, fellow author Upton Sinclair demurred: 'That the work of a drinker who had no intention of stopping drinking should become a major propaganda piece in the campaign for Prohibition is surely one of the choice ironies in the history of alcohol.'[12] For adventure hunters, *John Barleycorn* has plenty of action. The book's most rousing episodes include spirited chapters on his teenage boozing and oyster-pirating shenanigans. These episodes do little to encourage temperance, but they definitely deliver ripping good yarns of drunken sprees and the jocular male bonding they engender. For artists, it affords inside information on the evolution of a successful writer. And for the celebrity hounds (and biographers), London reveals, and sometimes exaggerates, his working-class beginnings and relays how he beat the odds to become a rich and famous writer.

The book's latter chapters are particularly compelling in their haunted portrayal of London's quest for meaning in a post-Darwinian universe disenchanted by modern scientific rationalism. How does one impose meaning and value on such an insentient, uncaring universe? The starting point of London's quest and his epistemological dilemma parallels historian Yuval Harari's naturalistic description of human existence: 'From a purely scientific viewpoint, human life has absolutely no meaning. Humans are the outcome of blind evolutionary processes that operate without goal or purpose. Our actions are not part of some divine cosmic plan . . . Hence *any* meaning people ascribe to their lives is just a delusion.'[13] In *John Barleycorn*, London calls such delusions 'vital lies'.[14] These lies are 'normal' or secondary truths – the healthy, comforting illusions we resign ourselves to, even though, on some level, we know them to be false. As London concedes: 'Normal truth is a different order, and a lesser order, of truth.'[15] Conversely, the 'White Logic', which is induced by heavy drinking, reveals a higher order of truth than the consoling illusions of 'vital lies'.[16] Spurred on and compounded by alcohol, the White Logic is an 'argent messenger of truth beyond truth, the antithesis of life, cruel and bleak as interstellar space, pulseless and frozen as absolute zero, dazzling with the frost of irrefragable logic and unforgettable fact'. London asserts that 'John Barleycorn will not let the dreamer dream, the liver live. He destroys birth and death, and dissipates to mist the paradox of being, until his victim cries out . . . "Our life's a cheat, our death a black abyss."'[17] It is not a stretch to suggest that, philosophically at least, London was a mean drunk.

John Barleycorn may grant a clear vision of first-order truth, but the White Logic that inevitably accompanies this perspective only intensifies the strain of existential bleakness that beckons one towards the oblivion of the abyss. 'Alcohol tells truth, but its truth is not normal. What is normal is healthful. What is healthful tends toward life.'[18] London knows that 'to be afraid is to be healthy. Fear of death makes for life. But the curse of the White Logic is that it does not make one afraid. The world-sickness of the White Logic makes one grin jocosely into the face of the Noseless One [death].'[19]

London claims that it was 'love, socialism, the PEOPLE – healthful figments of man's mind' that drew him out of the nihilistic pit of his existential crisis induced by the White Logic.[20] This recovery from his 'long sickness' would have occurred some time after his separation from Bess, and certainly his affair with Charmian had an ameliorating effect, but it is difficult to believe that he was ever as fully 'cured' as he claims in *John Barleycorn*. Yes, life was worth living, but the truth-seeker in London knew that our vital lies, though pragmatic, were still delusions.

He finished *John Barleycorn* on 4 January 1913, and the coming year, beleaguered by misfortune and distress, would severely test his resistance to the White Logic. 'My face', he wrote, 'changed forever in that year of 1913.'[21] An early frost destroyed some of his fruit crops, grasshopper swarms devastated his fledgling eucalyptus groves, hot winds and drought scorched his corn crops and a prized brood mare was killed by a stray hunter's bullet. He was embroiled in another legal battle over the motion picture copyrights of his works. He also made disastrous investments in Mexican land stocks, a lithograph company and a loan and mortgage company. In July, he underwent an appendectomy. He quickly recovered from the surgery, but during the procedure his physician, William S. Porter, discovered that London's kidneys were seriously diseased. The kidney damage was most likely caused or exacerbated by the liberal doses of corrosive sublimate he had used to treat his yaws on the *Snark* cruise. Dr Porter recommended that he cut down on meat and include more fruits and vegetables in his diet, but London did little to reform his eating habits. In his last three years of life, his health was in continual decline. His incessant smoking, dental problems and periodontal disease, and, most detrimentally, his deteriorating kidneys all contributed to various health issues, including hypertension, oedema and bloating, kidney stones and prostate problems, joint pain and rheumatism.

The next month brought another severe disappointment. On 22 August 1913 his nearly completed dream home on the ranch, known as Wolf House, was destroyed by fire. He had been especially passionate about its construction, which had begun back in April 1911, and the Londons were weeks away from moving in when it caught fire. Designed by San Francisco architect Albert Farr, the home's rustic organicism and stately magnitude were the architectural expression of London's personality and his aesthetic vision. Built on a knoll with a magnificent view of Sonoma Valley, the house fused Adirondack and Art and Crafts styles. The 1,400-square-metre (15,000 sq. ft) U-shaped design featured a reflecting pool fed by a mountain stream, and the four-storey, 26-room structure was made of boulders, blue slate, concrete and irregular-shaped volcanic rock blasted from a local quarry. It sat on an earthquake-resistant foundation adequate to support a 40-storey building. The roof was Spanish tile and the interior featured redwood panelling

Photograph of architect Albert Farr's rendering of the exterior of Jack London's Wolf House.

Ruins of the Wolf House, 2011.

and beams of rough-hewn logs. The home had electricity and refrigeration, and the bathrooms were state of the art. Charmian commented that Wolf House should not be thought of 'as a mansion, but as a big cabin, a lofty lodge, a hospitable tepee, where [London], simple and generous despite all his baffling intricacy, could stretch himself and beam upon you and me and all the world that gathered by his log fires'.[22] He wanted a home of 'air, sunshine, and laughter', so the main rooms were open and expansive.[23] The two-storied, 5.5 x 18 metre (18 x 58 ft) living room was the central gathering space and the dining room could seat fifty people. The home also featured a special writing room for London on the fourth level, perched above a capacious library room. The basement level included a 'Stag Party Room', a lavish early twentieth-century specimen of a 'man cave'.

London suspected that a disgruntled worker may have set the blaze, but a 1995 forensic investigation determined that the fire was caused by the spontaneous combustion of linseed-oil-soaked rags that workers had carelessly piled in a corner.[24] The blaze totally gutted the structure. The catastrophic damage reduced Wolf House to a skeleton of cement and stone within a few hours. Publicly, London was a model of stoic endurance, but privately he was dejected. He planned to rebuild Wolf House, but died before he got the chance. Today, as part of Jack London State Historic Park, the moss-coated stone ruins of Wolf House still stand, austere and otherworldly, in a copse of maples, redwoods and manzanitas.

The home's destruction was a major setback for the ranch, but he pushed forward with other new developments. In 1914 he was busy overseeing the building of concrete silos and relocated a blacksmith shop from the town of Glen Ellen to the ranch grounds. He also designed and constructed a circular, labour-saving piggery, which locals jokingly dubbed the 'pig palace'. The circular design, however, was innovative, efficient and labour saving.

His aspirations for the ranch were beginning to coalesce, but, as a remarried divorcee, he was struggling as a father in his emotional relationships with his daughters, Joan and Becky. He dutifully – though sometimes peevishly – provided Bess and the girls with a house in Oakland and financial support, but he had had difficulty establishing a deeper emotional rapport with his daughters as they matured. As young children, Joan and Becky had adored their father, but he was more of an abstract romantic figure who was almost entirely absent from their day-to-day lives. Unfortunately, he and Bess had few cultural precedents to guide their own conduct as divorced parents, and their disagreements inevitably created emotional stress for their daughters. His conflicts with Bess distracted him from his parental responsibilities, and both parents had a tendency to offload their emotional frustrations with each other onto their children. Considerable difficulty stemmed from the fact that London did not visit or see his daughters very often. In addition, Bess refused to let Joan and Becky visit the ranch because she did not want them to have any contact with Charmian, whom she deemed a morally compromised individual. Despite his physical and emotional absence for much of their lives, London loved his daughters and endured much emotional distress due to their repeatedly strained and infrequent interactions.

His correspondence with Joan exposes serious parental shortcomings and outbursts of emotional abuse. Sounding as if he were arguing with an adult, London lashed out cruelly when he wrote to the then twelve-year-old Joan in 1913 about her visiting the ranch:

> Now Joan. Remember that the world is populated by big people . . . If you join with your mother in this little sex jealousy of a thwarted female, you will doom yourself to grow up in the little environment of the little place called Piedmont, which is populated by little people. On the other hand, I offer you the big things of the world; the big things that big people live and know and think and act.[25]

Joan, to her credit – or perhaps abetted by her mother – wrote back: 'I am perfectly satisfied with my present surroundings and do not wish to change them. I resent your opinions of my mother . . . She is a good mother, and what is greater in this world, than a good mother?'[26] Tensions and conflicts with Joan and her mother continued, but lessened somewhat towards the end of London's life.

In January 1914 he travelled to New York City to reclaim his ownership of the dramatic rights to *The Sea-Wolf*. The trip was prompted by a recent court ruling that had determined that ownership of dramatic rights also included the motion picture rights. Though film production was still in its earliest stages, London had already recognized the cinematic potential of his works in the rapidly developing movie industry and was determined not to lose out on any earnings from film adaptations of his writings. Negotiations took weeks, and he ended up paying $3,835 to reclaim the rights. In 1914 alone, Bosworth Inc. filmed versions of *John Barleycorn, The Valley of the Moon, Martin Eden* and *Burning Daylight*.[27]

Before he returned to Glen Ellen in late February, London had one particularly dicey night out on the town while still in New York. After attending a show at a Harlem burlesque club, he was in a taxi going down Broadway with his fellow revellers (a theatre manager and two showgirls from the club) when their taxi crashed and rolled. London got a mouthful of glass, was pinned under the vehicle and had to be pulled out of the wreckage by the police. After he and his companions were extricated from the wreckage, they refused medical treatment and bolted from the scene. They managed to speed away in another taxi, narrowly avoiding being identified by the press.[28]

Over the next few months on Beauty Ranch, he supervised the building of a new barn and carriage shed. He also constructed a dam to create an irrigation reservoir that doubled as a swimming lake. Nearby, a bathhouse was added for bathers and boaters, and he stocked the lake with 1,500 catfish.[29] By the end of March he had also completed a speculative novel entitled *The Star Rover*, one of his most singular works. The story is narrated by a former professor of agronomy named Darrell Standing, who is awaiting execution in a California prison. Standing was originally sentenced to life in prison for murder, but was given the death penalty after striking a prison guard. London had been an advocate for penal reform since his dismal experience in the Erie County Penitentiary, and, in part, the book is a protest against the death penalty and the brutal policies and practices in California prisons, where inmates were regularly bound in straitjackets and subjected to solitary confinement. For his alleged role in a prison escape plot, Standing endures mistreatment by the warden and penitentiary personnel by being bound in the 'jacket' for extended periods. To survive this tortuous form of confinement, he claims to have developed techniques of 'astral projection' that allow him to 'star rove' back through time and relive his past-life identities. Embedded throughout Standing's present-day prison narrative are seven accounts of his previous incarnations as Count Guillaume de Sainte-Maure, a Renaissance French courtier and swordsman; Jesse Fancher, an American pioneer boy who dies in the 1857 Mountain Meadows Massacre; a nameless fourth-century Christian ascetic who lives in an Egyptian cave; Adam Strang, a European who, after a shipwreck, winds up in Korea, where he is tangled in the intrigues of the royal court; Ragnar Lodbrog, a Dane who becomes a legion officer in the Roman army and witnesses the crucifixion of Jesus; Daniel Foss, a seaman marooned for eight years on a desert island in the South Pacific; and, lastly, a composite sequence of incarnations that reaches back into pre-history and follows the ascent of humanity through the ages and across cultures: 'I, Darrell Standing, have rehearsed and relived all that primitive man was, and did, and became until he became even you and me and the rest of our kind in a twentieth century civilization.'[30] The prison and astral projection elements allow London to string together a series of tales that are basically self-contained short stories, but the assorted stories are partially unified through recurring motifs of dislocation and isolation.

London claimed not to be a believer in astral travel, but asserted: 'The key-note of the book is THE SPIRIT TRIUMPHANT.'[31] Another major motif is the triumph of the imagination. Nothing in the novel substantiates the actual validity of Standing's 'star roving' claims, and his narrative dependability is questionable. A crafty variation on the 'vital lies' London wrote about in *John Barleycorn*, it seems that Standing's astral travels are actually expedient and effective creative delusions – a psycho-imaginative survival mechanism that enable Standing to endure his suffering, confinement, guilt and impending execution.[32] In Standing's mind, astral travel confirms the immortality of his spirit, which he believes will go on to occupy a never-ending series of physical bodies across time and space. 'The spirit only is real,' he declaims. 'The flesh is phantasmagoric and apparitional.'[33] At one point, he rails at the court officials who condemn him: 'The fools! As if they could throttle my immortality with their clumsy device of rope and scaffold! I shall walk, and walk again, oh, countless times, this fair earth. And I shall walk in the flesh, be prince and peasant, savant and fool, sit in the high place and groan under the wheel.'[34] Imagination is the great escape in *The Star Rover*.

In late April 1914, London travelled to Veracruz to report on the Mexican Revolution for *Collier's* magazine. He arrived too late to witness any combat and was eventually laid low by amoebic dysentery at the end of May. Along with his fellow socialists, he had previously supported the revolution, but what he saw on the ground in Mexico prompted him to shift his support in favour of the American military intervention, which was deployed to protect U.S. corporate oil interests. His volte-face was based on first-hand experience but his views infuriated socialists bent on propping up Marxist ideology. What drew London's ire was his observation that the supposed revolutionaries had implemented despotic and inhumane tactics similar to those of their former oppressors.

That April, London also started writing *The Little Lady of the Big House*, which would be the last of his novels published before his death. Set on a sprawling Sonoma ranch, the book centres on Dick and Paula Forrest, a married couple who in many respects resemble Jack and Charmian. Thematically, the narrative ranges widely. While it examines agrarianism and male identity, it also explores matters of love, sex and adultery. The challenges of maintaining an intimate relationship in the context of marriage are at the narrative's thematic core. Dick Forrest embodies many of London's own personal excesses and failings as a husband. Obsessed with efficiency, production and profits, Dick is a rank workaholic, a neglectful husband and something of a self-absorbed narcissist. Paula must bear the brunt of Dick's disregard and ends up having a brief affair with Evan Graham, one of Dick's old friends, whose emotional sensitivities and attentiveness to Paula contrast sharply with Dick's selfish and mechanized existence. Jeanne Campbell Reesman observes that London 'intends to present Dick Forrest with a sense of irony and, at times, even contempt',[35] and Charles Watson Jr sees the novel as 'a story of middle age and loss. Despite its title, it is the story principally of Dick Forrest, a supreme rationalist and pragmatist whose tragic illusion is that life can be planned and controlled – that by an act of will he can create and preserve a marital Eden and an agricultural utopia.'[36] Because London saddles the plot with a plethora of ideas – Darwinism, existentialism and livestock breeding are also recurring subjects – its narrative pace is not particularly enthralling, but the novel is his most nuanced exploration of marriage and one of his most incisive critiques of masculinity.

In January 1915 the Londons sailed the *Roamer* up the Sacramento River to Stockton, and then travelled overland to Truckee for some winter fun. Physically, London was in bad shape. His legs and feet were habitually swollen and he was suffering from chronic gout, which kept him from ice skating or skiing. These ailments were symptomatic of his ailing kidneys and a failing urinary system. To deal with the pain, he continued to take morphine, which was legal at the time and was a drug he had regularly been using since the summer of 1908. As was the norm, London self-injected with a hypodermic needle.

To help assuage the author's various ailments, the Londons and Nakata left on the steamer *Matsonia* for Hawaii's salubrious climate on 24 February. They stayed on Waikiki Beach and frequented the Outrigger Club. London wrote regularly but engaged in little physical activity. He spent most afternoons lounging around in his kimono and relaxing on the beach in the shade with Charmian. He read, played cards, dozed in a hammock and attended evening luaus and other social gatherings. Though nothing could prevent London's diminishing health, the gentle climate and subdued ambience of the islands did put him more at ease. He worked steadily on two new dog novels, *Jerry of the Islands* and *Michael, Brother of Jerry*. Though these novels are little read today, London's Preface to *Michael* turned out to be a significantly influential protest piece against the widespread abuses inflicted by trainers on animals that performed in the vaudeville acts and variety shows popular during the era. After London's death, the preface inspired the formation of an international network of animal humane societies called Jack London Clubs. The clubs worked to expose instances of animal cruelty and their boycotts virtually put an end to vaudeville-style animal acts.

On 16 July the Londons left Honolulu and returned to Beauty Ranch, where they entertained numerous guests and friends who visited throughout that summer and autumn. London liked giving his visitors tours of the ranch, and he forged ahead with his various agricultural and livestock projects. After a few months in California, the Londons were eager to return to Hawaii and left on 16 December for an extended seven-month stay in the islands. Once more, they were captivated by Hawaii's idyllic beauty and enjoyed

Jack and Charmian London on the beach at Waikiki, Hawaii, 1915.

the laid-back social atmosphere. While island life assuaged the pains of London's chronic uraemia, he also went through the excruciating pain of passing kidney stones, an ordeal that would repeat itself several more times before his death. London was also becoming increasingly dismayed over the cataclysm of the First World War, and on 7 March 1916 he resigned from the Socialist Party.

Writing from Honolulu to members of the Local Glen Ellen Socialist Labor Party, he stated, 'I am resigning from the Socialist

Party because of its lack of fire and fight, and its loss of emphasis on the class struggle . . . Since the whole trend of socialism in the United States of recent years has been one of peaceableness and compromise, I find that my mind refuses further sanction of my remaining a member.'[37] He was not resigning because he no longer believed in the cause, but because he believed the Party itself was not socialist *enough*; that is, they had bypassed the commitment to revolution in favour of appeasement and concession to the bourgeois-capitalist powers-that-be. In the letter, he went on to question the ability and resolve of the proletariat to achieve their basic revolutionary objectives. 'If races and classes cannot rise up,' he continued, 'and by their own strength of brain and brawn wrest from the world liberty, freedom and independence, they never, in time, can come to these royal possessions.'[38] The letter reflects some of the same socio-political anxieties he had dramatized in *The Iron Heel*, and his professed reasons for resignation highlights his feeling that the working class was being being bribed into economic compromise by an elite capitalist minority set on maintaining its dominant status for the long term.

Though unstated in the letter, his pro-ally position in regard to the First World War, which had been raging since the summer of 1914, was factored into his decision. The Party had adopted what was, in essence, an anti-interventionist position, which London found reprehensible. 'I believe', he declared in late August 1916, 'intensely in the pro-ally side of the war. I believe that the foundation of civilization rests on the pledge, the agreement, and the contract. I believe the present great war is being fought out to determine whether or not men in the future may continue in a civilized way to depend upon the word, the pledge, the agreement, and the contract.'[39]

London's prolonged stays in Hawaii had also influenced his views on cultural diversity. On his previous visit in April 1915 he had first given a lecture entitled 'The Language of the Tribe', which encouraged cross-cultural understanding and cooperation through the formation of a Pan-Pacific Union. This club would be a gathering place where peoples of the diverse nations and races of Asia and Oceania, the Americas, Europe and elsewhere could 'meet each other and learn to understand each other'.[40] It would be a setting 'where men of all races can come, where they can eat together and smoke together and talk together'.[41] He stressed: 'There is nothing Utopian about [the club], the facts are all in its favor, and this world language has no better chance for a start than right now, here in our Hawaii, where the people of all the countries that rest around the edge of the Pacific meet.'[42] He delivered the speech several times, and his promotion helped to establish the Pan-Pacific Union. In part, London was promoting Hawaii as a tourist destination, but he was also beginning to appreciate the positive features of globalization, multiculturalism and racial integration.

He was fascinated by Polynesian mythology and his experiences on the *Snark* combined with his exposure to the complexities of Hawaii's cultural diversity animated much of his later Pacific fiction. The mingling of Oceanic cultures refreshed and extended many of the themes and ideas he had been addressing throughout his career. These late works tend to focus on intercultural tensions, and he often portrays the ways in which the primal, mythic qualities of traditional cultures are under siege by a demythologized Western rationalism. The stories 'The Bones of Kahekili', 'Shin Bones' and 'The Tears of Ah Kim', collected in *On the Makaloa Mat*, all focus on social frictions that emerge as Western cultural values and technology begin to infiltrate the lives of indigenous residents. In many ways, these conflicts were also externalized manifestations of the turmoil that swirled within London's own perpetually conflicted psyche. He was a visionary storyteller, who regularly drew on the uncanny upwellings from a mysterious inner demon; yet, his worldview had also been moulded by the principles of the Enlightenment, biology and modern philosophy. He was drawn to non-rational 'truths' that were imagined through myth, fable and ritual. At the same time, he had difficulty disregarding the modern empirically oriented belief that 'truth' was limited to things that could be calculated, measured and dissected.

These oppositions are evoked in one of the strangest and most distinguished of London's late stories, 'The Red One'. Written in May 1916, this tale follows the quest of Bassett, a British scientist and butterfly collector on the island of Guadalcanal in the Solomons, who is drawn inland through jungles and across grasslands by a euphonically mystifying sound that resonates from somewhere in the island's interior. He likens the sound to 'the mighty cry of some Titan of the Elder World' that seems 'to covey some cosmic secret, some understanding of infinite import and value'.[43] Bassett, the modern scientist, is bent on deciphering that 'cosmic secret'. Moving 'deeper and deeper into the mysterious heart of the unexplored island' he is wracked by fever and thirst, and on the brink of death is saved by the bushwoman Balata. She escorts him to her village where he meets Ngurn, the local medicine man who is also a zealous collector of human heads. Ngurn controls access to the Red One – the entity that generates the enormous sound – a 'perfect sphere, fully two hundred feet in diameter'.[44] The sphere is apparently a probe or vessel from outer space fashioned by advanced extraterrestrials. Balata secretly enables Bassett to see the Red One, which to him seems an interstellar 'messenger between the worlds', and he likens it to a giant shimmering 'cherry-red' pearl.[45] As Bassett nears death, Ngurn permits him access to the Red One in the moments before the medicine man beheads him. Bassett's final visions are wondrous but inconclusive. In the presence of the Red One he is 'lost in ecstasy at the abrupt and thunderous liberation of sound' and 'in that moment the interstices of matter were his . . . the interfusings and intermating transfusings of matter and force'.[46] His rapturous communion is euphoric, but in the instant before his decapitation the vision shifts, and Bassett 'gaze[s] upon the serene face of the Medusa, Truth'.[47] Is this foreboding image the reality of ultimate truth? And what does the Red One represent? London's big red sphere is enticingly ambiguous. Scholars have seen the Red One as an archetypal symbol of wholeness and completion, but it also radiates a sinister, powerful and otherworldly force.[48] Weirdly, the Red One is simultaneously primeval and highly evolved. It could represent the self, the soul, humanity, the alien or the universe. It might suggest humanity's need to fuse the primordial and instinctual with the modern and the rational.[49] The Red One's indeterminacy could also signify the fundamental inscrutability of life and humanity's inability to obtain a systematized explanation of existence. Or perhaps it implies the presence of some yet undiscovered perceptual paradigm beyond shamanism and science that could elucidate humanity's relation to the essential mystery of life, its origins and its ultimate purposes. Enigmatic and irreducible, the Red One is an exceptionally beguiling symbol.

The last short story London wrote, 'The Water Baby', provides another example of an epistemological conflict in London's portrayal of the white rationalist John Lakana (London's Hawaiian name) and Kohokumu, an elderly Hawaiian. During a fishing expedition, Kohokumu regales Lakana with Polynesian myths and fables. Lakana, a jaded cynic and materialist, questions Kohokumu's resolute acceptance of the Maui myth – 'And you believe all this?'[50] A discussion of myth and religion follows, and Kohokumu's graceful defence of mythical meanings outplays Lakana's world-weary adherence to a sceptical empiricism. The validity of Kohokumu's views is also embodied through his robust physical vigour and psycho-spiritual exuberance, which contrast sharply with the younger Lakana's exhaustion and discontent. Kohokumu informs Lakana: 'But listen, O Young wise One, to my elderly wisdom, This I know: as I grow old I seek less from the truth without me, and find more of the Truth from within me.'[51]

The unfinished novel London was working on when he died, *Cherry*, similarly highlights the complexities of cross-cultural understanding. Here, he tells the story of a Japanese orphan adopted in her infancy by a well-to-do white family of the Hawaiian planter class. In his notes for the novel, London wrote:

> Wealthy couple adopt pretty Japanese baby . . . Educated, refined, above par of white girls of same class. Peculiarly Beautiful . . . Problem: What was to become of her? Who would marry her? . . . She was essentially sensitive, artistic, a creator of beauty in her own way, also an emotional genius . . . in spite of training, upbringing, etc., was the baffling enigma of the oriental mind . . . Motif: Desire for understanding; baffling enigma of her own mind; and call of kind. Be sure to elaborate her Japanese traits.[52]

Her racial otherness in relation to her family and to multi-ethnic Hawaii gives her a unique perspective on the local population:

> Perhaps it was because of her very alienness of race, but at any rate she had thought much and was consciously more aware of the ten thousand nuances that differentiate the Hawaii folk from all other folk, than were the Hawaii folk themselves consciously aware . . . She understood, even what they could not understand of themselves.[53]

London even goes so far as to imbue Cherry with a dose of her own ethno-cultural pride: 'Only to herself privily, did she ever contemplate the naked thought that a thousand years back of the date when all of them (white, brown or tan) were screaming savages, her race had developed the arts, sciences, and refinements of intercourse.'[54] Lawrence Philips comments that '*Cherry* skillfully captures the tensions in prestatehood Hawai'ian society and its dilemmas, while simultaneously exploring the nature of European-style colonialism and looking at the geographical rivalry between the United States and the Japanese empire in the Pacific.'[55] It may have been a creative reach – or a function of his own cultural arrogance – for London to depict Cherry's subjectivity, but the novel demonstrates an attempt to comprehend and sympathize with a perspective very different from his own.

At a luau on 25 July 1916, attended by forty Hawaiian friends in his honour, London was recognized by locals as a *kamaaina*, 'a child of the land'. The next day, the Londons departed for California on the *Matsonia* and were back in Oakland on 1 August. London and Charmian attended the State Fair in Sacramento in early September, where their shorthorn bull 'Roselawn Choice' and their shire stallion 'Neuadd Hillside' won Grand Championships.[56] At the fair, London's left foot became so inflamed and arthritic that he was unable to walk and had to spend a week in bed. Such bouts of 'rheumatism' were symptomatic of his chronic and ever worsening uraemia. His foot improved, but Neuadd Hillside died suddenly back at the ranch on 22 October.[57] The prize stallion's death profoundly distressed London. In the first part of November, London had to take the stand in a court case involving water rights and a dam he had built that affected the flow of a creek to nearby properties below the ranch. London won the case, but his multiple court appearances were physically and emotionally taxing. He continued to work on his novel *Cherry*, and had completed five stories since his return from Hawaii.

He was planning to meet with his British publisher in New York City in late November to discuss future writing projects, but on the morning of 22 November London was found in a comatose state in his bed at 7.45 a.m. His face was a dark blue colour and his breathing was laboured. Eliza and Charmian frantically tried to revive him. Medical doctors Allan Thomson and Wilfred Hays arrived at approximately 8 a.m.[58] Finding empty vials of morphine on the floor, Thomson – who was unaware of London's kidney condition – suspected morphine poisoning.[59] Assisted by Charmian and Eliza, Thomson administered potassium

Grave site of Jack London, 1916.

permanganate gastric lavages, injected 50 cc of atropine and performed artificial respiration, along with vigorous body rubs.[60] Nothing worked. London's personal physician, Dr William S. Porter, arrived mid-afternoon from Oakland, but the author never emerged from his unresponsive state and died at 7.45 p.m. London was forty years old. The cause of death listed by Dr Porter on the death certificate was 'Uraemia [blood poisoning due to kidney failure] following renal colic [kidney stones].'[61] Porter cited 'Chronic Interstitial Nephritis of 3 years duration' as a contributing factor.[62]

That evening, Charmian wrote in her dairy: 'Day of alternate despair and the losing fight at the end when he beat us out and went into the great dark with a smile on his face – the smile he wanted to wear at the finish and the sun goes down.'[63] London's body was cremated in Oakland. Back at Beauty Ranch on 26 November his remains were laid to rest in a simple ceremony on a knoll not far from the ruins of Wolf House. The urn containing his ashes was buried under a massive volcanic rock that had been deemed too large in the construction of Wolf House.

# References

1 Western Youth: Born into the Underclass (1875–88)

1 Benson Bobrick, *The Fated Sky: Astrology in History* (New York, 2005), p. 7.
2 Jack London, 'How I Became a Socialist' [1905], in *Jack London: Novels and Social Writings*, ed. Donald Pizer (New York, 1982), p. 1117.
3 Russ Kingman, *A Pictorial Life of Jack London* (New York, 1979), p. 18.
4 Ibid., p. 20.
5 Ibid., pp. 15–16.
6 Ibid., pp. 17–18.
7 Ibid., p. 20.
8 Family members other than Flora who believed Chaney was the father included London's second wife Charmian Kittredge London, his daughter (and future biographer) Joan, his stepsister Eliza Shepard, and his step-nephew Irving Shepard.
9 Quoted in Clarice Stasz, *Jack London's Women* (Amherst, MA, 2001), p. 9.
10 Joseph Noel, *Footloose in Arcadia* (New York, 1940), p. 17.
11 Jeanne Campbell Reesman, *Jack London's Racial Lives: A Critical Biography* (Athens, GA, 2009), p. 309, n. 24.
12 Earle Labor, Robert C. Leitz III and I. Milo Shepard, eds, *The Letters of Jack London* (Stanford, CA, 1988), vol. I, p. 148.
13 Clarice Stasz, 'Families Friends, Mentors', in *The Oxford Handbook of Jack London*, ed. Jay Williams (New York, 2017), p. 42.
14 Stasz, *Jack London's Women*, p. 17.
15 Quoted in Charmian London, *The Book of Jack London* [1921] (Orinda, CA, 2018), vol. I, p. 24.
16 Ibid., p. 29.
17 Jack London, 'What Life Means to Me' [1909], in *The Portable Jack London*, ed. Earle Labor (New York, 1994), p. 475.

18  Labor et al., *Letters*, vol. i, p. 24.
19  Jack London, *White Fang* [1906], in *Jack London: Novels and Stories*, ed. Donald Pizer (New York, 1982), p. 153.
20  Joan London, *Jack London and His Times: An Unconventional Biography* [1939] (Seattle, WA, 1968), p. 2.
21  C. London, *Book*, vol. i, p. 30.
22  Jack London, *John Barleycorn* [1913], in *Novels and Social Writings*, p. 946.
23  Ibid., p. 942.
24  Ibid., p. 943.
25  Labor et al., *Letters*, vol. i, p. 148.
26  Ibid., vol. iii, p. 1392.
27  George Wharton James, 'A Study of Jack London in his Prime', in *Overland Monthly*, LXIX (1916), pp. 366–7.
28  Ibid., p. 367.
29  Labor et al., *Letters*, vol. i, p. 149.
30  Ibid., vol. iii, p. 1392.
31  London, *Barleycorn*, p. 954.
32  Frank Atherton, *Jack London in Boyhood Adventures* (Scotts Valley, CA, 2014), pp. 13–14.
33  Ibid., p. 17.
34  Ibid., p. 58.
35  Ibid., p. 61.
36  Ibid., p. 109.
37  Ibid., p. 110.
38  Earle Labor, *Jack London: An American Life* (New York, 2013), p. 32.
39  Jack London, 'The Joy of Small-boat Sailing' [1911], in *The Cruise of the Snark* [1911], ed. R. D. Madison (New York, 2004), p. 254.
40  C. London, *Book*, vol. i, p. 31.

2  Desperado: Wharf Rat, Oyster Pirate, Road Kid (1889–92)

1  Jack London, *John Barleycorn* [1913], in *Jack London: Novels and Social Writings*, ed. Donald Pizer (New York, 1982), p. 991.
2  Lord Byron, *The Corsair* [1814], in *Lord Byron: The Complete Poetical Works*, ed. Jerome McGann (New York, 1981), vol. iii, p. 150.

3 London, *Barleycorn*, p. 957.

4 Ibid.

5 Ibid., p. 958.

6 Ibid.

7 Ibid., p. 959.

8 Ibid., p. 960.

9 Ibid., p. 961.

10 Ibid., p. 960.

11 Ibid.

12 Ibid., p. 962.

13 Ibid.

14 Ibid., p. 963.

15 Ibid.

16 Charmian London, *The Book of Jack London* [1921] (Orinda, CA, 2018), vol. I, p. 56.

17 London, *Barleycorn*, pp. 954–5.

18 Ibid., p. 955.

19 Ibid.

20 Ibid., p. 965.

21 Jack London, 'The Apostate' [1911], in *Jack London: Novels and Stories*, ed. Donald Pizer (New York, 1982), p. 801.

22 Ibid., p. 811.

23 Ibid., p. 805.

24 Ibid., p. 965.

25 Ibid., p. 966.

26 Ibid., p. 983.

27 Ibid., p. 975.

28 Ibid., p. 974.

29 Ibid., p. 975.

30 Ibid., p. 974.

31 Ibid., p. 977.

32 Ibid., p. 978.

33 Frank Atherton, *Jack London in Boyhood Adventures* (Scotts Valley, CA, 2014), p. 190.

34 Ibid.

35 Ibid.

36 Jack London, *The Cruise of the Dazzler* [1902] (Orinda, CA, 2018), pp. 17, 8.

37 Ibid., pp. 153–4.
38 Retired California Game Warden Website and Blog, http:// californiawarden.com/history, accessed 2 August 2020.
39 London, *Barleycorn*, p. 992.
40 Ibid., p. 993.
41 Jack London, *The Road* [1907], in *Novels and Social Writings*, p. 278.
42 Ibid.
43 Ibid., p. 281.
44 Ibid., p. 278.
45 Ibid.
46 London, *Barleycorn*, p. 1000.
47 Ibid., p. 1007.
48 Ibid.
49 Ibid., p. 1008.

3  Young Adventurer: Pacific Sailor and American Tramp (1893–4)

1   Jack London, 'That Dead Men Rise Up Never', in *The Human Drift* [1917] (Orinda, CA, 2018), p. 38.
2   Charmian London, *The Book of Jack London* [1921] (Orinda, CA, 2018), vol. I, p. 81.
3   Jack London, *John Barleycorn* [1913], in *Jack London: Novels and Social Writings*, ed. Donald Pizer (New York, 1982), p. 992.
4   Quoted in C. London, *Book*, vol. I, pp. 91–2.
5   Ibid., p. 93.
6   London, 'Dead Men', p. 34.
7   Ibid., p. 36.
8   Ibid., pp. 35–6.
9   London, *Barleycorn*, pp. 1009–10.
10  Ibid., p. 1010.
11  Ibid., p. 1013.
12  John Sutherland, 'Appendix 1: Jack London and the *Sophia Sutherland*', in *The Sea-Wolf* (Oxford, 1992), p. 332.
13  Ibid., p. 334.
14  Jack London, *The Sea-Wolf* [1904], in *Jack London: Novels and Stories*, ed. Donald Pizer (New York, 1982), p. 603.

15  London, *Barleycorn*, p. 1023.
16  Ibid.
17  Ibid., p. 1026.
18  Quoted in Jay Williams, *Author Under Sail: The Imagination of Jack London, 1893–1902* (Lincoln, NE, 2014), p. 34.
19  London, *Barleycorn*, p. 1032.
20  Jack London, 'What Life Means to Me' [1906], in *The Portable Jack London*, ed. Earle Labor (New York, 1994), p. 477.
21  Jack London, 'The Somnambulists', in *Revolution and Other Essays* [1910] (Orinda, CA, 2018), p. 36.
22  Jack London, *The Tramp Diary*, in *Jack London on the Road: The Tramp Diary and Other Hobo Writings*, ed. Richard W. Etulain (Logan, UT, 1979), p. 54.
23  Ibid.
24  Daniel Dyer, *Jack London: A Biography* (New York, 1997), p. 44.
25  Jack London, *The Road* [1907], in *Novels and Social Writings*, p. 233.
26  Ibid., p. 232.
27  Quoted in Russ Kingman, *A Pictorial Life of Jack London* (New York, 1979), p. 55.
28  London, *The Road*, p. 253.
29  Ibid., pp. 252–3.
30  Ibid., p. 248.
31  Ibid., pp. 248–9.
32  Ibid., p. 193.
33  Ibid., pp. 193–4.
34  Ibid., p. 194.
35  London, *Barleycorn*, p. 1039.
36  Ibid., pp. 1039–40.
37  Jack London, 'How I Became a Socialist' [1905], in *Novels and Social Writings*, p. 1119.
38  Ibid., p. 1040.
39  Ibid., p. 1119.
40  Ibid., p. 1120.

4  Epic Stampede: From Student to Klondike Gold Rusher
(1894–8)

1  *Jack London by Himself*, Promotional Pamphlet (New York, n.d.).
2  Jack London, 'In a Far Country' [1910], in *Jack London: Novels and Stories*, ed. Donald Pizer (New York, 1982), p. 308.
3  Earle Labor, *Jack London: An American Life* (New York, 2013), p. 80.
4  Georgia Loring Bamford, *The Mystery of Jack London: Some of his Friends, Also a Few Letters: A Reminiscence* (Oakland, CA, 1931), p. 21.
5  Jack London, 'What Socialism Is', in *The Radical Jack London: Writings on War and Revolution*, ed. Jonah Raskin (Berkeley, CA, 2008), p. 57.
6  Phil Gasper, *The Communist Manifesto: A Road Map to History's Most Important Political Document* (Chicago, IL, 2005), p. 212.
7  Joan London, *Jack London and His Times: An Unconventional Biography* [1939] (Seattle, WA, 1968), p. 378.
8  Jack London, *John Barleycorn* [1913], in *Jack London: Novels and Social Writings*, ed. Donald Pizer (New York, 1982), pp. 1043–4.
9  Ibid., p. 1044.
10  Quoted in Russ Kingman, *A Pictorial Life of Jack London* (New York, 1979), p. 67.
11  Ibid., p. 68.
12  London, *Barleycorn*, p. 1049.
13  In September 1897, London's story 'Two Gold Bricks' did appear in *Owl* magazine, but he never got word that it had been published. See Jay Williams, *Author Under Sail: The Imagination of Jack London, 1893–1902* (Lincoln, NE, 2014), p. 97.
14  Joan London, *Jack London and His Times*, p. 135.
15  Kingman, *Pictorial*, p. 70.
16  Charmian London, *The Book of Jack London* [1921] (Orinda, CA, 2018), p. 189.
17  London, *Barleycorn*, p. 1054.
18  Franklin Walker, *Jack London and the Klondike: The Genesis of an American Writer* [1966] (San Marino, CA, 1994), p. 83.
19  Jack London, 'Through the Rapids on the Way to the Klondike' [1899], https://thegrandarchive.wordpress.com, accessed 2 December 2019.
20  Ibid.
21  Ibid.

22 Jack London, *The Call of the Wild* [1903], in *Novels and Stories*, pp. 33–4.

23 Jack London, *The Cruise of the Snark* [1911], ed. R. D. Madison (New York, 2004), p. 11.

24 Marshall Bond, 'Marshall Bond's Eulogy on Jack London 1916', www. jack-london.org, accessed 1 September 2019.

25 Ibid.

26 Quoted in C. London, *Book*, vol. I, p. 195.

27 Quoted in Walker, *Jack London and the Klondike*, pp. 111–12.

28 Quoted ibid., p. 137.

29 Russ Kingman, *Jack London: A Definitive Chronology* (Middletown, CA, 1992), p. 18.

30 Jack London, 'From Dawson to the Sea' [1899], https:// thegrandarchive.wordpress.com, accessed 1 September 2019.

31 Quoted in Mike Wilson, *Jack London's Klondike Adventure* (Sonoma, CA, 1995), p. 113.

32 Renato Rosaldo, *Culture and Truth: The Remaking of Social Analysis* [1989] (Boston, MA, 1993), p. 69.

33 Quoted in Walker, *Jack London and the Klondike*, p. 176.

34 London, *Barleycorn*, p. 1054.

## 5 Writer at Work: Early Success, Love, Marriage (1898–1902)

1 Earle Labor, Robert C. Leitz III and I. Milo Shepard, eds, *The Letters of Jack London* (Stanford, CA, 1988), vol. II, p. 976.

2 Walt Whitman, *Leaves of Grass: The First (1855) Edition* [1855], ed. Malcolm Cowley (New York, 1961), p. 85.

3 Johnny Miller was the son of John London's daughter Ida London Miller, whose husband had abandoned her.

4 Jack London, *John Barleycorn* [1913], in *Jack London: Novels and Social Writings*, ed. Donald Pizer (New York, 1982), p. 1056.

5 Jack London, 'What Life Means to Me' [1906], in *The Portable Jack London*, ed. Earle Labor (New York, 1994), p. 478.

6 Labor et al., *Letters*, vol. I, p. 59.

7 Ibid., p. 164.

8 Jay Williams, *Author Under Sail: The Imagination of Jack London, 1893–1902* (Lincoln, NE, 2014), p. 4.

9  Jack London, 'Again the Literary Aspirant' [1902], in *No Mentor but Myself: Jack London on Writing and Writers*, ed. Dale Walker and Jeanne Reesman (Stanford, CA, 1999), p. 49.

10  Labor et al., *Letters*, vol. I, p. 137.

11  Ibid., p. 26.

12  Ibid., p. 31.

13  Ibid., p. 32.

14  Williams, *Author Under Sail*, p. 137.

15  Russ Kingman, *Jack London: A Definitive Chronology* (Middletown, CA, 1992), p. 24.

16  Williams, *Author Under Sail*, p. 134.

17  Clarice Stasz, *Jack London's Women* (Amherst, MA, 2001), p. 50.

18  Labor et al., *Letters*, vol. I, p. 329.

19  Jack London, 'The White Silence' [1900], in *Jack London: Novels and Stories*, ed. Donald Pizer (New York, 1982), pp. 300–301.

20  Jack London, 'Amateur Night' [1906], in *The Complete Short Stories of Jack London*, ed. Earle Labor, Robert C. Leitz III and I. Milo Shepard (Stanford, CA, 1993), vol. II, p. 716.

21  Jack London, 'Local Color' [1906], in *Complete Short Stories*, p. 690.

22  Labor et al., *Letters*, vol. I, p. 328.

23  Ibid., vol. I, p. 329.

24  Jack London, 'On the Writer's Philosophy of Life' [1899], in *Portable Jack London*, p. 426.

25  Ibid., p. 427.

26  Ibid., p. 429.

27  Ibid.

28  Quoted in Eric Miles Williamson, *Oakland, Jack London, and Me* (Huntsville, TX, 2007), p. 5.

29  Quoted in Russ Kingman, *A Pictorial Life of Jack London* (New York, 1979), p. 90.

30  Kenneth K. Brandt, *Jack London: Writers and Their Work* (Liverpool, 2018), p. 4.

31  Labor et al., *Letters*, vol. I, p. 19.

32  Ibid.

33  Dan Wichlan, '1916, A Thousand Words A Day', The Jack London Society 13th Biennial Symposium. Unpublished conference paper. (Napa Valley College, CA, September 2016).

34  Jay Williams, 'What did Jack London Earn?', *The Call: The Magazine of the Jack London Society*, xx/2 (Fall/Winter 2009), p. 7.

35  Jacqueline Tavernier-Courbin, 'Jack London and Anna Strunsky: Lovers at Cross-purposes', in *Jack London: One Hundred Years a Writer*, ed. Sara S. Hodson and Jeanne Campbell Reesman (San Marino, CA, 2002), pp. 21–2.

36  Joseph Noel, *Footloose in Arcadia* (New York, 1940), p. 147.

37  Quoted in Tavernier-Courbin, 'London and Strunsky', p. 24.

38  Stasz, *Jack London's Women*, p. 61.

39  Labor et al., *Letters*, vol. I, p. 178.

40  Stasz, *Jack London's Women*, p. 61.

41  Labor et al., *Letters*, vol. I, p. 239.

42  Ibid., vol. I, p. 267, n. 2.

43  Jack London and Anna Strunsky, *The Kempton-Wace Letters* [1903] (Orinda, CA, 2018), pp. 67, 69.

44  Ibid., p. 161.

45  Earle Labor, *Jack London: An American Life* (New York, 2013), pp. 162–3.

46  Charmian London, *The Book of Jack London* [1921] (Orinda, CA, 2018), vol. I, p. 318.

47  Jack London, *The People of the Abyss* [1903], in *Novels and Social Writings*, p. 164.

48  Labor et al., *Letters*, vol. I, p. 306.

49  London, *People of the Abyss*, p. 166.

50  Agnes Malinowska, 'From Atavistic Gutter-wolves to Anglo-Saxon Wolf: Evolution and Technology in Jack London's Urban Industrial Modernity', in *The Oxford Handbook of Jack London*, ed. Jay Williams (New York, 2017), p. 440.

51  C. London, *Book*, vol. I, p. 319.

52  London, *People of the Abyss*, pp. 181–2.

53  Ibid., p. 181.

54  Williams, *Author Under Sail*, p. 553.

55  Labor et al., *Letters*, vol. I, p. 342.

56  Ibid., vol. I, p. 351.

6 *The Call of the Wild*: Celebrity, War, Divorce, Fame, Remarriage (1903–6)

1   Earle Labor, Robert C. Leitz III and I. Milo Shepard, eds, *The Letters of Jack London* (Stanford, CA, 1988), vol. I, p. 366.
2   Ibid., p. 318.
3   Jack London, *The Call of the Wild* [1903], in *Jack London: Novels and Stories*, ed. Donald Pizer (New York, 1982), p. 36.
4   Quoted in Joan R. Sherman, *Jack London: A Reference Guide* (Boston, MA, 1977), p. 14.
5   Donald Pizer, 'Jack London: The Problem of Form', in *Bloom's Modern Critical Views: Jack London*, ed. Harold Bloom (New York, 2011), p. 6.
6   Abraham Rothberg, 'Introduction', in *The Call of the Wild* [1903] and *White Fang* [1906] (New York, 1984), p. 9.
7   Earle Labor and Jeanne Campbell Reesman, *Jack London: Revised Edition* (New York, 1994), p. 41.
8   Jacqueline Tavernier-Courbin, *The Call of the Wild: A Naturalistic Romance* (New York, 1994), p. 96.
9   Ibid., p. 99.
10  Michael Lundblad, 'The Nature of the Beast in *The Call of the Wild*', in *Approaches to Teaching the Works of Jack London*, ed. Kenneth K. Brandt and Jeanne Campbell Reesman (New York, 2015), pp. 156–7.
11  London, *Call of the Wild*, p. 35.
12  Ibid., p. 34.
13  Ibid., pp. 77–8.
14  Ibid., p. 77.
15  Iris Jamahl Dunkle, *Charmian Kittredge London: Trailblazer, Author, Adventurer* (Norman, OK, 2020), pp. 64–71.
16  Labor et al., *Letters*, vol. I, p. 522.
17  Ibid., p. 371.
18  Russ Kingman, *Jack London: A Definitive Chronology* (Middletown, CA, 1992), p. 45.
19  Labor et al., *Letters*, vol. I, p. 411.
20  Ibid., p. 413.
21  Kingman, *Chronology*, p. 49.
22  Labor et al., *Letters*, vol. I, p. 421.

23  Jack London, 'Japan Puts End to Usefulness of Correspondents', in *Jack London Reports*, ed. King Hendricks and Irving Shepard (Garden City, NY, 1970), p. 123.
24  Ibid., p. 122.
25  Labor et al., *Letters*, vol. I, p. 427.
26  Ibid., p. 427.
27  Daniel A. Métraux, *The Asian Writings of Jack London* (Lewiston, NY, 2009), p. 93.
28  See ibid., pp. iii–viii, 93–6.
29  Sherman, *Reference*, p. 30.
30  Ibid., p. 21.
31  Keith Newlin, 'Teaching Ideas in The Sea-Wolf ', in *Approaches to Teaching the Works of Jack London*, p. 36.
32  Jack London, *The Sea-Wolf* [1904], in *Novels and Stories*, p. 543.
33  Ibid., p. 534.
34  Ibid., p. 543.
35  Quoted in 'Commentary', in *The Sea-Wolf* (New York, 2000), p. 293.
36  Ibid., p. 520.
37  London, *The Sea-Wolf*, in *Novels and Stories*, p. 520.
38  Ibid.
39  Greg Forter, 'F. Scott Fitzgerald, Modernist Studies, and Fin-de-siècle Crisis in Masculinity', *American Literature*, LXXVIII/2 (2006), pp. 296–7.
40  London, *Sea-Wolf*, p. 500.
41  Labor et al., *Letters*, vol. I, p. 371.
42  Ibid.
43  Russ Kingman, *A Pictorial Life of Jack London* (New York, 1979), p. 144.
44  Daniel Dyer, *Jack London: A Biography* (New York, 1997), p. 152.
45  Kingman, *Chronology*, p. 70.
46  Labor et al., *Letters*, vol. I, p. 454.
47  Quoted in George Wharton James, 'A Study of Jack London in his Prime', *Overland Monthly*, LXIX (1916), p. 382.
48  Ibid.
49  Jack London, *White Fang* [1906], in *Novels and Stories*, p. 144.
50  Ibid., pp. 241–2.

## 7 To Build a Boat: The *Snark* Voyage, Hawaii, the South Seas (1907–9)

1 Jack London, *The Cruise of the Snark* [1911], ed. R. D. Madison (New York, 2004), p. 10.
2 'The Long Trail', quoted as epigraph, ibid., p. 6.
3 London, *Cruise*, p. 16.
4 Earle Labor, Robert C. Leitz III and I. Milo Shepard, eds, *The Letters of Jack London* (Stanford, CA, 1988), vol. II, p. 549.
5 Ibid., p. 548.
6 Ibid.
7 London, *Cruise*, p. 10.
8 Ibid., p. 8.
9 Ibid.
10 Ibid.
11 Charmian London, *The Book of Jack London* [1921] (Orinda, CA, 2018), vol. II, p. 102.
12 London, *Cruise*, p. 9.
13 Ibid., p. 24.
14 Martin Johnson, *Through the South Seas with Jack London* (New York, 1913), p. 57.
15 Keith Newlin, 'Jack London: Sailor', www.boatus.com, accessed 2 December 2019.
16 London, *Cruise*, p. 15.
17 Russ Kingman, *Jack London: A Definitive Chronology* (Middletown, CA, 1992), p. 77.
18 London had written a much shorter young-adult version of 'To Build a Fire', which was published in *Youth's Companion*, LXXVI (29 May 1902), p. 375. See Labor et al., *Letters*, vol. II, pp. 777–8.
19 For a description of the connection between Lynch's *Three Years in the Klondike* and London's 'To Bulid a Fire', see David Mike Hamilton, *'Tools of My Trade': The Annotated Books in Jack London's Library* (Seattle, WA, 1986), p. 198.
20 Jack London, 'To Build a Fire' [1908], in *Jack London: Novels and Stories*, ed. Donald Pizer (New York, 1982), p. 462.
21 Ibid., p. 470.
22 Ibid., pp. 469–70.

23  Ibid., p. 478.
24  London, *Cruise*, p. 68.
25  Ibid.
26  Ibid., p. 69.
27  Ibid., pp. 93–4.
28  Ibid., p. 93.
29  Ibid., p. 94.
30  Ibid., p. 94.
31  Ibid., pp. 99–100.
32  Ibid., p. 106.
33  Justin D. Edwards, *Exotic Journeys: Exploring the Erotics of u.s. Travel Literature, 1840–1930* (Hanover, NH, 2001), p. 54.
34  Ibid., p. 49.
35  Jack London, 'Koolau the Leper' [1911], in *Novels and Stories*, p. 462.
36  Ibid., p. 897.
37  London, *Cruise*, p. 110.
38  Ibid., p. 115.
39  Ibid., p. 118.
40  Edward B. Clark, 'Roosevelt on the Nature Fakirs', *Everybody's Magazine*, XVI (June 1907), pp. 770–74.
41  Jack London, 'The Other Animals' [1908], in *No Mentor but Myself: Jack London on Writing and Writers*, ed. Dale L. Walker and Jeanne Campbell Reesman (Stanford, CA, 1999), p. 110.
42  Ibid., p. 115.
43  London, *Cruise*, p. 129.
44  Labor et al., *Letters*, vol. III, p. 1398.
45  Kingman, *Chronology*, p. 89.
46  Ibid., pp. 89–90.
47  London, *Cruise*, p. 183.
48  Ibid., pp. 183–5.
49  Kingman, *Chronology*, p. 90.
50  London, *Cruise*, p. 173.
51  A. Grove Day, *Jack London in the South Seas* (New York, 1971), pp. 144–5.
52  Charmian London, *The Log of the Snark* (New York, 1915), p. 421.
53  London, *Cruise*, p. 168.
54  Quoted in C. London, *Book*, vol. II, p. 141.
55  Frank Praetorius, 'Jack London and Ross River Disease on the *Snark*

Voyage', *The Call: The Magazine of the Jack London Society*, XXIII/1–2 (2012), p. 17.

## 8 Back to the Land: Beauty Ranch and California (1909–12)

1 Earle Labor, Robert C. Leitz III and I. Milo Shepard, eds, *The Letters of Jack London* (Stanford, CA, 1988), vol. III, p. 1601.
2 Jack London, *Martin Eden* [1909], in *Jack London: Novels and Social Writings*, ed. Donald Pizer (New York, 1982), pp. 665–6.
3 Labor et al., *Letters*, vol. I, p. 489.
4 Homer L. Haughey and Connie Kale Johnson, *Jack London: Ranch Album* (Stockton, CA, 1985), p. 13.
5 Quoted in Charmian London, *The Book of Jack London* [1921] (Orinda, CA, 2018), vol. II, p. 219.
6 Labor et al., *Letters*, vol. III, p. 1601.
7 Ibid., p. 1378.
8 Haughey and Johnson, *Ranch Album*, p. 35.
9 Labor et al., *Letters*, vol. II, p. 813.
10 Ibid., p. 667.
11 Ibid., p. 569.
12 Ibid., p. 644.
13 London, *Martin Eden*, p. 814.
14 Ibid., p. 816.
15 Ibid., p. 908.
16 Ibid., pp. 894, 916.
17 Ibid., p. 917.
18 Ibid., p. 930.
19 Ibid., p. 931.
20 Jack London, *Burning Daylight* [1910] (Orinda, CA, 2018), p. 121.
21 Ibid., pp. 6–7.
22 Ibid., p. 30.
23 Ibid., p. 29.
24 Ibid., p. 173.
25 Ibid., p. 194.
26 Ibid., p. 295.
27 Ibid., p. 339.

28  Ibid., p. 340.
29  Ibid., p. 317.
30  Ibid., pp. 315–16.
31  Ibid., p. 123.
32  Ibid., p. 323.
33  Ibid., p. 344.
34  Ibid., p. 378.
35  Ibid., p. 262.
36  Labor et al., *Letters*, vol. II, p. 909, n. 1.
37  London's short story 'The Benefit of the Doubt', included in *The Night-born* (New York, 1913), is based on the incident.
38  Earle Labor, *Jack London: An American Life* (New York, 2013), p. 313.
39  Jeanne Campbell Reesman, 'London, Jack Johnson, and the "Great White Hope"', in *Critical Insights: Jack London*, ed. Lawrence I. Berkove (Pasadena, CA, 2012), p. 344.
40  Jack London, 'Jeffries–Johnson Fight', in *Jack London Reports*, ed. King Hendricks and Irving Shepard (Garden City, NY, 1970), p. 293.
41  Ibid., p. 301.
42  Quoted in C. London, *Book*, vol. II, p. 160.
43  Ibid., p. 163.
44  Jack London, 'Four Horses and a Sailor', in *The Human Drift* [1917] (Orinda, CA, 2018), p. 66.
45  C. London, *Book*, vol. II, p. 163.
46  Ibid., p. 167.
47  Labor, *American Life*, p. 321.
48  C. London, *Book*, vol. II, pp. 172–3.
49  Quoted in James L. Haley, *Wolf: The Lives of Jack London* (New York, 2010), p. 277.
50  Joseph Noel, *Footloose in Arcadia* (New York, 1940), p. 221.
51  Quoted in Clarice Stasz, *American Dreamers: Charmian and Jack London* (New York, 1988), p. 234.
52  Quoted in C. London, *Book*, vol. II, p. 195.

## 9 Cosmos Mariner: Final Travels and Last Days (1912–16)

1 'Jack London's Credo', *The Jack London Online Collection* (Sonoma State University), http://london.sonoma.edu, accessed 3 December 2019.

2 Cormac McCarthy, *The Crossing* (New York, 1994), p. 45.

3 Quoted in Iris Dunkle, 'Previously Unpublished Selections from "The Log of the *Dirigo*"', *Women's Studies*, XLVI/4 (2017), p. 402.

4 Ibid., p. 405.

5 Jack London, *The Valley of the Moon* [1913] (Orinda, CA, 2018), p. 405.

6 Ibid., pp. 385–6.

7 Earle Labor, Robert C. Leitz III and I. Milo Shepard, eds, *The Letters of Jack London* (Stanford, CA, 1988), vol. II, p. 1008.

8 Russ Kingman, *Jack London: A Definitive Chronology* (Middletown, CA, 1992), p. 149.

9 Quoted in Russ Kingman, *A Pictorial Life of Jack London* (New York, 1979), p. 242.

10 Labor et al., *Letters*, vol. III, p. 1484.

11 Jeanne Campbell Reesman, *Critical Companion to Jack London: A Literary Reference to His Life and Work* (New York, 2011), p. 132.

12 Upton Sinclair, *The Cup of Fury* [1956] (Westwood, NJ, 1965), p. 136.

13 Yuval N. Harari, *Sapiens: A Brief History of Humankind* (New York, 2015), p. 391.

14 Jack London, *John Barleycorn* [1913], in *Jack London: Novels and Social Writings*, ed. Donald Pizer (New York, 1982), p. 937.

15 Ibid., p. 1093.

16 Ibid., p. 939.

17 Ibid., p. 1094.

18 Ibid., p. 1093.

19 Ibid., p. 1097.

20 Ibid., p. 1067.

21 Quoted in Charmian London, *The Book of Jack London* [1921] (Orinda, CA, 2018), vol. II, p. 210.

22 Ibid., p. 218.

23 Quoted in Elisa Stancil Levine, *Jack London State Historic Park* (Charleston, SC, 2015), p. 38.

24 'Origin of the Wolf House Fire: Dr Robert Anderson's Forensic Group

Study', in Gregory W. Hayes and Matt Atkinson, *Jack London's Wolf House* (Glen Ellen, CA, 2010), pp. 42–5.

25  Labor et al., *Letters*, vol. III, pp. 1258–9.

26  Ibid., p. 1260, no. 2.

27  Kingman, *Chronology*, p. 174.

28  Labor et al., *Letters*, vol. III, p. 1296.

29  Kingman, *Pictorial*, p. 251.

30  Jack London, *The Star Rover* [1915] (Orinda, CA, 2018), p. 290.

31  Labor et al., *Letters*, vol. III, p. 1315.

32  Kenneth K. Brandt, *Jack London: Writers and Their Work* (Liverpool, 2018), pp. 99–105.

33  London, *Star Rover*, p. 161.

34  Ibid., p. 30.

35  Reesman, *Critical Companion*, p. 160.

36  Charles N. Watson, Jr, *The Novels of Jack London: A Reappraisal* (Madison, WI, 1983), p. 219.

37  Labor et al., *Letters*, vol. III, pp. 1537, 1538.

38  Ibid.

39  Ibid., vol. III, p. 1571.

40  Jack London, 'The Language of the Tribe', in *Jack London: The Unpublished and Uncollected Articles and Essays*, 3rd edn, ed. Daniel J. Wichlan (Scotts Valley, CA , 2018), p. 284.

41  Ibid., p. 281.

42  Ibid.

43  Jack London, 'The Red One' [1918], in *Jack London: Novels and Stories*, ed. Donald Pizer (New York, 1982), p. 966.

44  Ibid., p. 981.

45  Ibid., pp. 987, 981.

46  Ibid., p. 990.

47  Ibid.

48  See Jeanne Campbell Reesman, *Jack London: A Study of the Short Fiction* (New York, 1999), pp. 161–70.

49  Brandt, *Jack London*, pp. 117–20.

50  Jack London, 'The Water Baby' [1918], in *Novels and Stories*, p. 955.

51  Ibid., p. 960.

52  Quoted in Earle Labor, *Jack London: An American Life* (New York, 2013), pp. 373–4.

53  Jack London, *Cherry*, ed. Tony Williams, *Jack London Journal*, VI (1999), p. 42.

54  Ibid.

55  Lawrence Phillips, '*Cherry*, Unfinished Business', in *The Oxford Handbook of Jack London*, ed. Jay Williams (New York, 2017), pp. 418–19.

56  Kingman, *Chronology*, p. 222.

57  Ibid., p. 224.

58  Richard M. Rocco, 'The Medical Treatment of Jack London on the Day that he Died: November 22, 1916', *The Call: The Magazine of the Jack London Society*, XXIX/2–3 (2018–19), p. 8.

59  In *Pictorial*, Kingman notes: 'It is understandable that Dr Thomson erred in his diagnosis. Seeing Jack in a coma and a morphine vial on the floor . . . he concluded that Jack had taken an overdose, an opinion based on circumstances rather than medical evidence' (pp. 273–4). Kingman also states: 'It was highly possible that in the throes of his terrible suffering he had taken extra doses of the morphine prescription given to him by Dr Porter to ease his agony. It was possible that the extra morphine was a contributory factor, but the coma was induced by retention of bodily poisons his inoperative kidneys could no longer release' (ibid., p. 273).

60  Rocco, 'Medical Treatment', p. 9.

61  Quoted ibid., p. 8.

62  Ibid.

63  Quoted in Kingman, *Chronology*, p. 224.

# Select Bibliography

Works by Jack London

Novels

*The Cruise of the Dazzler* (New York, 1902)
*A Daughter of the Snows* (Philadelphia, PA, 1902)
*The Call of the Wild* (New York, 1903)
*The Kempton-Wace Letters* [with Anna Strunsky] (New York, 1903)
*The Sea-Wolf* (New York, 1904)
*The Game* (New York, 1905)
*White Fang* (New York, 1906)
*Before Adam* (New York, 1907)
*The Iron Heel* (New York, 1908)
*Martin Eden* (New York, 1909)
*Burning Daylight* (New York, 1910)
*Adventure* (New York, 1911)
*The Abysmal Brute* (New York, 1913)
*The Valley of the Moon* (New York, 1913)
*The Mutiny of the Elsinore* (New York, 1914)
*The Scarlet Plague* (New York, 1915)
*The Star Rover* (New York, 1915)
*The Little Lady of the Big House* (New York, 1916)
*Jerry of the Islands* (New York, 1917)
*Michael, Brother of Jerry* (New York, 1917)
*Hearts of Three* (New York, 1920)
*The Assassination Bureau* [completed by Robert L. Fish] (New York, 1963)
*Cherry* [unfinished novel by Jack London], ed. Tony Williams, *Jack London Journal*, VI (1999), pp. 4–76

Non-fiction and Memoir

*The People of the Abyss* (New York, 1903)
*War of the Classes* (New York, 1905)
*The Road* (New York, 1907)
*The Cruise of the Snark* (New York, 1911)
*John Barleycorn* (New York, 1913)


Short-story Collections

*The Son of the Wolf* (Boston, MA, 1900)
*The God of His Fathers and Other Stories* (New York, 1901)
*Children of the Frost* (New York, 1902)
*The Faith of Men and Other Stories* (New York, 1904)
*Tales of the Fish Patrol* (New York, 1905)
*Moon-face and Other Stories* (New York, 1906)
*Love of Life and Other Stories* (New York, 1907)
*Lost Face* (New York, 1910)
*South Sea Tales* (New York, 1911)
*When God Laughs and Other Stories* (New York, 1911)
*The House of Pride and Other Tales of Hawaii* (New York, 1912)
*Smoke Bellew* (New York, 1912)
*A Son of the Sun* (Garden City, NY, 1912)
*The Night-born* (New York, 1913)
*The Strength of the Strong* (New York, 1914)
*The Turtles of Tasman* (New York, 1916)
*The Red One* (New York, 1918)
*On the Makaloa Mat* (New York, 1919)
*Dutch Courage and Other Stories* (New York, 1922)


Fiction, Non-fiction and Sketches

*Revolution and Other Essays* (New York, 1910)
*The Human Drift* [1917] (Orinda, CA, 2018)

Plays

*Scorn of Women* (New York, 1906)
*Theft: A Play in Four Acts* (New York, 1910)
*The Acorn-planter: A California Forest Play* (New York, 1916)
*The Birthmark,* in *The Human Drift* [1917] (Orinda, CA, 2018), pp. 137–66
*A Wicked Woman,* in *The Human Drift* [1917] (Orinda, CA, 2018), pp. 97–135


Anthologies and Collections of Works by Jack London

*The Complete Short Stories of Jack London*, ed. Earle Labor, Robert C. Leitz III
    and I. Milo Shepard, 3 vols (Stanford, CA, 1993)
*Jack London, American Rebel: A Collection of His Social Writings Together with an
    Extensive Study of the Man and His Times*, ed. Philip S. Foner (New York, 1947)
*Jack London: Novels and Social Writings*, ed. Donald Pizer (New York, 1982)
*Jack London: Novels and Stories*, ed. Donald Pizer (New York, 1982)
*Jack London Reports*, ed. King Hendricks and Irving Shepard (Garden City,
    NY, 1970)
*Jack London: The Unpublished and Uncollected Articles and Essays*, 3rd edn,
    ed. Dan Wichlan (Scotts Valley, CA, 2018)
*No Mentor but Myself: Jack London on Writing and Writers*, ed. Dale L. Walker
    and Jeanne Campbell Reesman (Stanford, CA, 1999)
*The Portable Jack London*, ed. Earle Labor (New York, 1994)
*The Radical Jack London: Writings on War and Revolution*, ed. Jonah Raskin
    (Berkeley, CA, 2008)


Correspondence

*The Letters of Jack London*, ed. Earle Labor et al., 3 vols (Stanford, CA, 1988)


Biographies

Dunkle, Iris Jamahl, *Charmian Kittredge London: Trailblazer, Author,
    Adventurer* (Norman, OK, 2020)

Kingman, Russ, *A Pictorial Life of Jack London* (New York, 1979)

Labor, Earle, *Jack London: An American Life* (New York, 2013)

London, Charmian, *The Book of Jack London* [1921], 2 vols (Orinda, CA, 2018)

London, Joan, *Jack London and His Times: An Unconventional Biography* [1939] (Seattle, WA, 1968)

Stasz, Clarice, *Jack London's Women* (Amherst, MA, 2001)

Viotte, Michel, with Noël Mauberret, *The Lives of Jack London*, trans. Jacqueline Dinsmore (Buffalo, NY, 2018)


Secondary Sources and Criticism

Adam, Philip, Jeanne Campbell Reesman and Sara S. Hodson, *Jack London, Photographer* (Athens, GA, 2010)

Berkove, Lawrence I., ed. *Critical Insights: Jack London* (Pasadena, CA, 2012)

Brandt, Kenneth K., *Jack London: Writers and Their Work* (Liverpool, 2018)

—, and Jeanne Campbell Reesman, eds, *Approaches to Teaching the Works of Jack London* (New York, 2015)

Cassuto, Leonard, and Jeanne Campbell Reesman, eds, *Rereading Jack London* (Stanford, CA, 1996)

Gair, Christopher, *Complicity and Resistance in Jack London's Novels: From Naturalism to Nature* (Lewiston, NY, 1997)

Hamilton, David Mike, *'Tools of My Trade': The Annotated Books in Jack London's Library* (Seattle, WA, 1986)

Hayes, Gregory W., and Matt Atkinson, *Jack London's Wolf House* (Glen Ellen, CA, 2010)

Hodson, Sara S., and Jeanne Campbell Reesman, eds, *Jack London: One Hundred Years a Writer* (San Marino, CA, 2002)

Kingman, Russ, *Jack London: A Definitive Chronology* (Middletown, CA, 1992)

Labor, Earle, and Jeanne Campbell Reesman, *Jack London: Revised Edition* (New York, 1994)

Levine, Elisa Stancil, *Jack London State Historic Park* (Charleston, SC, 2015)

McAleer, Joseph, *Call of the Atlantic: Jack London's Publishing Odyssey Overseas, 1902–1916* (New York, 2016)

Newlin, Keith, ed., *The Oxford Handbook of American Literary Naturalism* (New York, 2011)

Nuernberg, Susan, ed., *The Critical Response to Jack London* (Westport, CT, 1995)

Reesman, Jeanne Campbell, *Critical Companion to Jack London: A Literary Reference to His Life and Work* (New York, 2011)

—, *Jack London: A Study of the Short Fiction* (New York, 1999)

—, *Jack London's Racial Lives: A Critical Biography* (Athens, GA, 2009)

Sherman, Joan R., *Jack London: A Reference Guide* (Boston, MA, 1977)

Tavernier-Courbin, Jacqueline, *The Call of the Wild: A Naturalistic Romance* (New York, 1994)

Tichi, Cecelia, *Jack London: A Writer's Fight for a Better America* (Chapel Hill, NC, 2015)

Walker, Franklin, *Jack London and the Klondike: The Genesis of an American Writer* [1966] (San Marino, CA, 1994)

Watson, Charles N. Jr, *The Novels of Jack London: A Reappraisal* (Madison, WI, 1983)

Williams, Jay, *Author Under Sail: The Imagination of Jack London, 1893–1902* (Lincoln, NE, 2014)

—, ed., *The Oxford Handbook of Jack London* (New York, 2017)

Special Journal Issues

*Eureka Studies in Teaching Short Fiction* [Jack London Issue], V/1 (Fall 2004)

*Modern Fiction Studies* [Jack London Issue], XXII/1 (Spring 1976)

*Studies in American Literary Naturalism* [Special Issue: Jack London and Ernest Hemingway], XI/1 (Summer 2016)

*Studies in American Literary Naturalism* [Special Issue: New Journeys along Jack London's *The Road*], XIV/1 (Summer 2019)

Other Publications and Websites

*The Call: The Magazine of the Jack London Society*, ed. Kenneth K. Brandt (1990–)

*The Jack London Journal*, ed. Jay Williams (1994–2000)

*The Jack London Online Collection* (Sonoma State University), https://london.sonoma.edu

*The Jack London Society: The Life and Work of Jack London*, https://jacklondonsociety.org

# Acknowledgements

For their gracious support and scholarly insights, I would like to thank Angela Brandt, Jeanne Campbell Reesman, Sara S. Hodson, Jay Williams, Penelope Krumm, Daniel Wichlan, Anita Duneer, Richard Rocco, Juan Gomez, Carl Bell and the members of the Jack London Society. Research for this volume was made possible by a generous grant from the Henry E. Huntington Library.

# Photo Acknowledgements

The author and publishers wish to express their thanks to the below sources of illustrative material and/or permission to reproduce it. Some locations of artworks are also given below, in the interest of brevity:

The Bancroft Library, University of California, Berkeley: pp. 16, 104, 159; photo Walter Bibikow, courtesy Jon Arnold Images Ltd/Alamy Stock Photo: p. 184 (foot); from W. H. Chaney, *Chaney's Primer of Astrology and American Urania* (St Louis, MO, 1890): p. 10; Jack London Papers, The Huntington Library, San Marino, CA: pp. 9, 12, 14, 20, 51, 55, 70, 83, 91, 98, 101, 103, 107, 117, 120, 123, 129, 137, 141, 144, 148, 151, 169, 171, 173, 179, 184 (top), 192, 199; Library of Congress, Prints and Photographs Division, Washington, DC: pp. 30, 62, 78; from Charmian London, *The Book of Jack London*, vol. II (New York, 1921): p. 6; from Jack London, *The Cruise of the Dazzler* (New York, 1902): p. 40; from Jack London, *John Barleycorn* (New York, 1913): p. 31; San Francisco Maritime National Historical Park, CA: p. 48; University of Washington Libraries, Seattle: p. 76.